NEW ENGLAND INST. OF TECHNOLOGY

W9-AQQ-043

HN 90 .M3 P66 2005

Popular culture

DATE DUE

NEW ENGLAND INSTITUTE OF TECHNOLOGY
LIBRARY

Popular
CULTURE

Opposing Viewpoints®

Other Books of Related Interest

Popular CULTURE

Opposing Viewpoints®

John Woodward, *Book Editor*

Bruce Glassman, *Vice President*
Bonnie Szumski, *Publisher*
Helen Cothran, *Managing Editor*

OPPOSING
VIEWPOINTS®
SERIES

GREENHAVEN PRESS
An imprint of Thomson Gale, a part of The Thomson Corporation

NEW ENGLAND INSTITUTE OF TECHNOLOGY
LIBRARY

THOMSON

━━━━━✦━━━━━™
GALE

Detroit • New York • San Francisco • San Diego • New Haven, Conn.
Waterville, Maine • London • Munich

8|06   #57465643

© 2005 Thomson Gale, a part of The Thomson Corporation.

Thomson and Star Logo are trademarks and Gale and Greenhaven Press are registered trademarks used herein under license.

For more information, contact
Greenhaven Press
27500 Drake Rd.
Farmington Hills, MI 48331-3535
Or you can visit our Internet site at http://www.gale.com

ALL RIGHTS RESERVED.
No part of this work covered by the copyright hereon may be reproduced or used in any form or by any means—graphic, electronic, or mechanical, including photocopying, recording, taping, Web distribution or information storage retrieval systems—without the written permission of the publisher.

Every effort has been made to trace the owners of copyrighted material.

Cover credits: © Photos.com, Stockbyte

LIBRARY OF CONGRESS CATALOGING-IN-PUBLICATION DATA
Popular culture : opposing viewpoints / John Woodward, book editor.
p. cm. — (Opposing viewpoints series)
Includes bibliographical references and index.
ISBN 0-7377-3105-2 (lib. : alk. paper) — ISBN 0-7377-3106-0 (pbk. : alk. paper)
1. Mass media—United States. 2. Violence in mass media—United States.
3. Popular culture—United States. 4. United States—Social conditions—1980– .
I. Woodward, John, 1958– . II. Opposing viewpoints series (Unnumbered)
HN90.M3P66 2005
302.23'0973—dc22   2005040223

Printed in the United States of America

"Congress shall make no law. . .abridging the freedom of speech, or of the press."

First Amendment to the U.S. Constitution

The basic foundation of our democracy is the First Amendment guarantee of freedom of expression. The Opposing Viewpoints Series is dedicated to the concept of this basic freedom and the idea that it is more important to practice it than to enshrine it.

Contents

Chapter 4: What Values Does Popular Culture Promote?

Why Consider Opposing Viewpoints?

"The only way in which a human being can make some approach to knowing the whole of a subject is by hearing what can be said about it by persons of every variety of opinion and studying all modes in which it can be looked at by every character of mind. No wise man ever acquired his wisdom in any mode but this."

John Stuart Mill

In our media-intensive culture it is not difficult to find differing opinions. Thousands of newspapers and magazines and dozens of radio and television talk shows resound with differing points of view. The difficulty lies in deciding which opinion to agree with and which "experts" seem the most credible. The more inundated we become with differing opinions and claims, the more essential it is to hone critical reading and thinking skills to evaluate these ideas. Opposing Viewpoints books address this problem directly by presenting stimulating debates that can be used to enhance and teach these skills. The varied opinions contained in each book examine many different aspects of a single issue. While examining these conveniently edited opposing views, readers can develop critical thinking skills such as the ability to compare and contrast authors' credibility, facts, argumentation styles, use of persuasive techniques, and other stylistic tools. In short, the Opposing Viewpoints Series is an ideal way to attain the higher-level thinking and reading skills so essential in a culture of diverse and contradictory opinions.

In addition to providing a tool for critical thinking, Opposing Viewpoints books challenge readers to question their own strongly held opinions and assumptions. Most people form their opinions on the basis of upbringing, peer pressure, and personal, cultural, or professional bias. By reading carefully balanced opposing views, readers must directly confront new ideas as well as the opinions of those with whom they disagree. This is not to simplistically argue that everyone who reads opposing views will—or should—change his or her opinion. Instead, the series enhances readers' understanding of their own views by encouraging confrontation with opposing ideas. Careful examination of others' views can lead to the readers' understanding of the logical inconsistencies in their own opinions, perspective on why they hold an opinion, and the consideration of the possibility that their opinion requires further evaluation.

Evaluating Other Opinions

To ensure that this type of examination occurs, Opposing Viewpoints books present all types of opinions. Prominent spokespeople on different sides of each issue as well as well-known professionals from many disciplines challenge the reader. An additional goal of the series is to provide a forum for other, less known, or even unpopular viewpoints. The opinion of an ordinary person who has had to make the decision to cut off life support from a terminally ill relative, for example, may be just as valuable and provide just as much insight as a medical ethicist's professional opinion. The editors have two additional purposes in including these less known views. One, the editors encourage readers to respect others' opinions—even when not enhanced by professional credibility. It is only by reading or listening to and objectively evaluating others' ideas that one can determine whether they are worthy of consideration. Two, the inclusion of such viewpoints encourages the important critical thinking skill of objectively evaluating an author's credentials and bias. This evaluation will illuminate an author's reasons for taking a particular stance on an issue and will aid in readers' evaluation of the author's ideas.

It is our hope that these books will give readers a deeper understanding of the issues debated and an appreciation of the complexity of even seemingly simple issues when good and honest people disagree. This awareness is particularly important in a democratic society such as ours in which people enter into public debate to determine the common good. Those with whom one disagrees should not be regarded as enemies but rather as people whose views deserve careful examination and may shed light on one's own.

Thomas Jefferson once said that "difference of opinion leads to inquiry, and inquiry to truth." Jefferson, a broadly educated man, argued that "if a nation expects to be ignorant and free . . . it expects what never was and never will be." As individuals and as a nation, it is imperative that we consider the opinions of others and examine them with skill and discernment. The Opposing Viewpoints Series is intended to help readers achieve this goal.

David L. Bender and Bruno Leone,
Founders

Greenhaven Press anthologies primarily consist of previously published material taken from a variety of sources, including periodicals, books, scholarly journals, newspapers, government documents, and position papers from private and public organizations. These original sources are often edited for length and to ensure their accessibility for a young adult audience. The anthology editors also change the original titles of these works in order to clearly present the main thesis of each viewpoint and to explicitly indicate the opinion presented in the viewpoint. These alterations are made in consideration of both the reading and comprehension levels of a young adult audience. Every effort is made to ensure that Greenhaven Press accurately reflects the original intent of the authors included in this anthology.

Introduction

"Technological innovation has changed the face of entertainment by drastically lowering the cost of production and distribution while increasing worldwide demand."
—Johanna Blakely, assistant director, Norman Lear Center
at the USC Annenberg School for Communication

The growth in influence of American popular culture throughout the world has been a direct result of technological advances—electrification of rural areas, and the creation of movies, television, CDs, and most recently, computers. In the nineteenth century people had to seek out popular entertainment in theaters, but with the advent of these new technologies in the twentieth century, access to popular culture increased dramatically.

Indeed, as the new technologies were perfected and became less expensive, they spread rapidly. In 1945 there were only 7,000 working TV sets in the United States and only 9 stations on the air; by 2001 there were 248 million TVs receiving programming from 1,937 broadcasting networks and stations. The personal computer did not exist in 1945; in 2001, 54 million American households had one or more computers, and most also had access to the Internet. The mass production of musical recordings, international distribution of films, delivery of television by satellite, and most recently, distribution of content on the Internet, have spread American popular culture throughout the world.

Although the United States is the only major industrialized nation not to have a minister of culture, its free-market approach to the creation of entertainment is more productive and successful than any state-funded program in the world. The typical European ministry of culture organizes and coordinates state culture and cultural-education policy, protects cultural heritage, and provides financial support to fledgling artists and entertainers. In contrast, while the United States does provide a relatively small amount of funding to artists through its National Endowment for the Arts, the vast majority of American popular culture is created by independent artists and businesses motivated by profit. This system has proved wildly successful. According to the Internet Movie Database, of the 252 movies that have earned more than $200 million, 196 are solely American made, and 48 are collaborations between foreign and American studios. These American movies were produced using private funds and represent the artistic vision of individual creators.

The reach of American popular culture includes more than just movies. U.S. television networks cover the world, as well. For example, CNN broadcasts to more than 200 of the 238 countries and territories; MTV reaches 176; Nickelodeon 162. American popular music also is widely influential throughout the world. In a typical week in June 2004, more than half of the top twenty songs on the music charts in both Australia and England were by American artists. Rap music performed by Americans is now popular and influential in countries as diverse as Italy and Jamaica.

Moreover, entertainment products created outside the United States can project American popular culture throughout the world. An example of this phenomenon is the hugely successful video game series, *Grand Theft Auto*, which features virtual cities based on places and periods well known to consumers of American films, television programs, and pop music: the Miami of the 1980s TV show *Miami Vice*, the South-Central Los Angeles of the 1990s movies *Boyz 'N the Hood* and *Colors*, and the gritty 1970s-era New York of countless movies and TV shows. The games were designed by Scotland-based Rockstar North.

In response to the omnipresence of American popular culture, a backlash has occurred. In 2002 the Pew Research Center surveyed thirty-eight thousand people in forty-four countries. They found that while American technology and popular culture were admired, "the spread of U.S. ideas and customs is disliked by majorities in almost every country included in the survey." This included even traditional allies such as Britain and Canada. Many countries outside the United States fear that America's export of popular culture— its popular books, films, music, and television—is threatening their unique ways of life. Local music, song, dance, drama, and folk culture are slowly being overwhelmed by the American pop culture monolith, they contend. Many even argue that the English language used by the American media is contributing to the slow extinction of indigenous languages throughout the world. Intellectuals in many European and Middle Eastern capitals use the word "McWorld" to describe what they perceive as the dumbing-down of their popular culture by American exports.

The growing influence of American popular culture is debated in *Opposing Viewpoints: Popular Culture* in the following chapters: Does Popular Culture Have Value? Is Popular Culture Too Coarse? Is Popular Culture Too Violent? What Values Does Popular Culture Promote? The diverse viewpoints in this anthology will help readers to understand the importance of examining popular culture and its role in the world. With the technological advances that have occurred in the twentieth century, that role has certainly increased, fueling the debate over popular culture's impact on society.

CHAPTER 1

Does Popular Culture Have Value?

Chapter Preface

The growing influence of rap music, video games, and reality TV place them at the center of popular culture, especially among youth, who generally drive trends in entertainment. As these media continue to grow in popularity, not surprisingly the controversies surrounding them have grown more vociferous. Detractors claim that these forms of entertainment not only lack redeeming value but are in fact harmful to society. On the other hand, supporters claim that rap music, video games, and reality TV are at worst harmless and at best beneficial. Regardless of where commentators stand on the issue, none can deny the growth of all three forms of entertainment in recent years.

According to the Recording Industry Association of America, in 1994 rock music dominated music sales with 35.1 percent of the market. Rap, then a newly emerging form, accounted for just 7.9 percent of recorded music sales. By 2003, however, rock sales had dropped by 28 percent to 25.2 percent while rap nearly doubled to 13.3 percent. The increase in sales of rap recordings was significant, especially when considering that a significant portion of its target demographic—young urban blacks—tend to have little disposable income to spend on entertainment. The pervasive influence of rap music and hip-hop culture is reflected in the fact that several rap performers have crossed over into other fields, such as acting, modeling, and fashion design. In addition, the clothing styles and slang associated with hip-hop culture pervade high school and college campuses.

Like rap music, video games also have become more popular. Video games increased in sales in the United States from $3.2 billion in 1995 to $6.9 billion in 2002, a more than 100 percent increase. While this increase can be partly attributed to the growth in personal computer and game console ownership in the United States, improvements in computer processing speed and video graphic cards have also played a role. The two top-selling video games of 2002 were also two of the most controversial: *Grand Theft Auto: Vice City* and *Grand Theft Auto III*. Despite claims that these products were too violent, the games, priced at about $50 each, sold millions of copies upon release and continue to sell well.

The popularity of reality TV has also grown. In the Fall 2004 television schedule for the six broadcast networks (ABC, CBS, NBC, Fox, UPN, and WB), the number of hours of traditional, scripted dramas and comedies declined from 73 to 63, the first such decline in TV history. Meanwhile, the number of hours devoted to reality programming doubled from 10 to 20. Participants in some reality shows have become as well known as famous actors, resulting in tremendous numbers of applicants wishing to participate in reality programs. For the 2004 edition of NBC's *The Apprentice*, over 1 million people applied for one of the few coveted spots.

Traditionally, new forms of entertainment appeal first to young people, with the new media being met with scorn and derision by older generations. This happened with jazz, movies, and rock music. Many analysts contend that a similar phenomenon is shaping the debate over rap music, video games, and reality TV. The viewpoints in this chapter examine whether these new forms of entertainment have redeeming value or whether they are dangerous to society.

"The process of getting to know the characters, of discovering the qualities and flaws that define them, and then discussing these discoveries with other viewers creates a simulation of community."

Reality TV Fosters Connections Between People

Heather Havrilesky

According to Heather Havrilesky in the following viewpoint, the reality TV genre is the most popular entertainment programming on television. She argues that the best reality TV shows feature more interesting characters than do traditional fictional TV programming. Viewers enjoy the process of getting to know the show participants and discussing developments with other people, Havrilesky points out. She concludes that reality TV shows promote a sense of community among those who watch them. Heather Havrilesky is Salon.com's TV critic.

As you read, consider the following questions:

1. According to the author, what are the weaknesses of current fictional dramas and comedies on television?
2. What qualities does Havrilesky believe separate the best reality TV shows from the worst?
3. What specific reality TV shows does the author criticize?

Heather Havrilesky, "Three Cheers for Reality TV," www.salon.com, September 13, 2004. Copyright © 2004 by Salon.com. Reproduced by permission.

"Sifting through so-called reality TV has become like rummaging through a landfill: There seems to be no end to the quantity and types of trash you'll find . . . If we're going to start setting taste standards for reality TV, there's going to be a lot of dead air time." [Myrtle Beach Sun News, 9/2/04]

"This is not just bad television in the sense that it's mediocre, pointless, puerile even. It's bad because it's damaging." BBC journalist John Humphrys, in a speech to U.K. TV executives [Reuters U.K., 8/27/04]

"Reality TV is so cheap because you don't need writers, actors, directors . . . it is killing off new talent and we are all worse off for that." Rebecca of Cambridge, U.K. [posting on BBC News, 8/28/04]

"Reality TV, in particular, mocks committed relationships and makes trust seem foolish, some teens said. So teens tend to 'hook up' with friends to get a sexual fix without the responsibility of a relationship." [Richmond Times-Dispatch, 9/7/04]

"Sarah Austin occasionally watches reality TV, but finds it sad, rather than engaging." [The Age, 9/5/04]

Welcome to the modern world, where we're all sucking on the same pop cultural crack pipe, but only the unrefined among us will admit that they inhale. Reality TV earns its reputation as the dangerous street drug du jour mostly by aiming its lens at human behavior—we're far less photogenic than we imagine ourselves to be. While shows run the gamut from high-quality, dramatically compelling work to silly, exploitative trash, pundits consistently point to programs at the bottom of the barrel and cast aspersions on those foolish enough to watch them. Thanks to this stigma, it's not always easy to get a clear picture of how many people genuinely enjoy reality shows and aren't about to give them up.

Instead, every few months, a new survey announces that reality is on its way out. Last March [2003], an *Insider Advantage* survey found that "67 percent of Americans" were "becoming tired of so-called reality programs." This year [2004], a survey by Circuit City concluded that 58 percent of viewers are "getting tired" of reality TV. (What are they excited about? Why, HDTV, of course—they just can't wait to purchase their new HDTV-capable sets!) Can you expect accurate results when you ask people if they're "getting tired" of anything? But even while many people take their cue from the media and bemoan the evils of reality, they're still watching. Just as there are those who claim to read *Penthouse* for the fine articles no matter how "sad, rather than engaging" reality TV might be, audiences have yet to drop off as predicted.

"Reality TV is not going away," says Marc Berman, television analyst for *Mediaweek*. "This summer, reality dominated. In terms of total viewers during the regular season, three of the top five shows ["The Apprentice," "American Idol" and "Survivor"] were reality shows." Berman predicts that we'll see these same reality shows pull in big numbers in the fall, along with frequent time-slot winners like "The Bachelor" and whichever new reality programs draw in big audiences. "The bottom line is that the genre is absolutely exploding," Berman says.

Instead of writing off millions of viewers as the unenlightened consumers of lowbrow entertainment, shouldn't we ask why they're attracted to reality TV in the first place?

Decline of Comedies and Dramas

First of all, viewers have been exposed to the same half-hour and hour episodic plot structures, implemented in roughly the same ways, for decades now, setting the stage for a less conventional format. Even once-groundbreaking, high-quality dramas like "ER" and "The West Wing" have evolved into parodies of themselves, with all the usual suspects striding through halls and corridors, spitting out the same clever quips until the next big tragedy hits. Meanwhile, traditional sitcoms are faring even worse, as the networks spend millions each fall to develop shows that don't stick. While those in the industry bemoan the fact that the networks have whittled their sitcom offerings down to two or three shows, that makes perfect sense when you recognize how bad TV executives have been at locating genuinely good shows, and how expensive it is just to develop a handful of episodes. "Two and a Half Men," one of the only new sitcoms from last fall to make it to another season, is considered a hit, yet it's not remotely funny. And the best sitcoms—"Everybody Loves Raymond," "Will & Grace" and "That '70s Show"—are all winding down, with one-half ("Raymond") to two years left in them, at most.

That's not to say that the world of scripted entertainment is dead—far from it. Instead, new formats are taking hold: one-camera sitcoms like "Arrested Development" and "Entourage," sketch comedies like "Chappelle's Show" and "Da Ali G Show," and unconventional twists on old formulas like "Deadwood" and "The Wire." But unconventional means risky, which is why none of those shows are on the Big Three networks, which seem as faithful to old-formula fiction . . .

Ultimately, though, it's not the basic format of the traditional sitcom or drama that's to blame, it's the lack of original, high-quality writing. By now everyone knows that HBO, a channel not poisoned by the copycat mentality of the networks, is behind most of the best shows on television. Many producers and writers report that quality scripts and ideas are out there, but the networks aren't necessarily looking for quality. What seems familiar about those wisecracking characters on their couches isn't the setting or the format, it's the mediocre jokes and story lines that simply mimic the story lines of other better—but not necessarily great—shows. Sadly, as the networks continue the impossible search for guaranteed hits and sure things, they limit their scope to the sorts of shows that have succeeded before instead of seeking original voices with something to say. This is why we'll end up watching soggy star vehicles like John Goodman's "Center of the Universe" and Jason Alexander's "Listen Up" (It worked with Charlie Sheen, right?) this fall [2004] instead of encountering truly original comedies with fresh, surprising characters.

What Reality Shows Offer

Will we be watching? The truth is, the best reality shows feature exactly the kinds of fresh, surprising characters that most sitcoms and dramas lack. For those who care about the quality of reality shows they produce, the bar has been set very high by Mark Burnett. At a time when reality TV appeared to be shackled to the somewhat shallow teenage-bitch-slap tradition of "The Real World," Burnett insisted on bringing the same intelligent editing and beautiful cinematography to "Survivor" that he brought to "Eco Challenge." He recognized that, beyond painstakingly careful casting and crafting of dramatically compelling story lines, viewers would want to get a real feel for the show's exotic setting. As fleeting as those aerial and wildlife shots can seem, they add an inestimable dimension to the viewer's experience. Anyone who watched the first few episodes of "Survivor" knew that the show was bound to be a hit, and the reason for that had more to do with sparkling shots of cornflower-blue water than it had to do with Richard Hatch (although having a naked, backstabbing provocateur around certainly helped).

Reality TV Helps Viewers Understand Life

Are these shows enlightening? Frequently. Take the grand-daddy of the reality genre, *Survivor*. . . . Along with the back-stabbing and political gamesmanship, part of the show's en-during appeal surely comes from watching recognizable types—various contestants who embody styles and personal strategies we have all encountered.

Life being the mess that it is, the consequences of real-life behavior can be frustratingly vague (or if displayed by the boss' offspring, nonexistent). In the intense world of the typical reality TV laboratory, consequences are not long in coming. It can be very satisfying.

Steve Burgess, "Forced to Watch: Reality TV," www.thetyee.ca, January 26, 2004.

If reality offerings were limited to claustrophobic, repetitive, aesthetically irritating shows like "Elimidate" or "The Bachelor," it would be easy to write off the entire genre as the work of sensationalistic producers churning out trash for a quick buck. Instead, a few sharp producers like Burnett saw the enormous potential of the form and approached it with a passion, creating a vicarious experience for the viewer. They recognized that reality TV could truly engage audiences, pulling them into a time and place, populated by real human beings. As long as the cast and the settings were a little larger than life, as long as the stories were edited to make the viewer feel like a personal confidante to each of the competitors, audiences would find themselves swept into the action, investing far more of their emotions in the competition than they imagined was possible.

"The Amazing Race" followed in the footsteps of "Survivor" in terms of quality, but conquered the most difficult production challenges imaginable. Ten teams of two scamper across the globe, racing to complete various tasks, but you never, ever spot a single camera, not when several teams are running across a beach to the finish line, not when they're hang gliding or walking teams of dogs or eating two pounds of Russian caviar. Produced by Jerry Bruckheimer and edited with so many suspense-inducing tricks it's impossible not to get caught up in the action, "The Amazing Race" took Burnett's high standards of human drama and visual appeal and built on them. Lumping together an intensely difficult, expensive, painstakingly produced show like "The Amazing Race" with meandering, silly shows like "The Ultimate Love Test" is an insult to the sharp, talented people who seem to set the bar higher each season.

Of course, meandering, silly shows have a certain charm of their own. Fox's "Paradise Hotel" stumbled on accidental genius with its hyperaggressive cast of frat boys and neurotics. Originally intended as a sleazy dating show where those guests who didn't "hook up" would get thrown out of Paradise *"forever!"* as the voice-over put it, "Paradise Hotel" evolved into a nasty battle between two cliques, with the producers scrambling to mold their "twists" and promos to fit the bizarre clashes arising on the set. There's something to be said for a show that evolves based on the strange behavior of its cast, thanks mostly to the fact that its cast is made up of belligerent drunks. Sadly, "Paradise Hotel's" success was purely accidental. The producers foolishly moved the show away from its original location, a gorgeous Mexican resort with brilliant white walls that lit every scene beautifully, making all of the inhabitants appear larger than life. They renamed the show, cast it with bland, empty-headed Neanderthals, added an even-more-awful host and some pointless twists, and the magic was over. The ironically titled "Forever Eden" was canceled before the season ended.

The Joy of Watching

But part of the joy of watching, for true reality aficionados, is witnessing such false starts and mesmerizingly entertaining mistakes. While those who've never seen much of the genre bemoan the foolishness of most shows, it's the newness of the form that makes it so exciting. When not even the producers can predict how the characters on a show will react, audiences feel like they're a part of something that's evolving before their eyes. The second season of "The Joe Schmo Show," titled "Joe Schmo 2," epitomized this state. The show lures two individuals into thinking that they're contestants on a dating show called "Last Chance for Love," when in fact, their fellow contestants are really actors, paid to create absurd, funny scenarios.

To the dismay of the show's producers and crew, a few episodes in, one of the two Schmos named Ingrid figured out that something was very wrong, and kept asking the actors around her if they had memorized the things they were saying, or if there was "some kind of 'Truman Show' thing going on." Instead of declaring the show a failure, the producers chose to reveal the truth to Ingrid and then enlisted her as an actor for the rest of the show. This kind of behind-the-scenes, seat-of-the-pants improvisation is such completely new territory, it's not hard to understand why audiences are intrigued.

Furthermore, if our obsession with celebrities tends to rise and fall and rise again in cycles, then it makes sense that reality TV would become popular in the wake of the late '90s, when celebrity obsession reached new levels of absurdity. Audiences bored with Brad and Jennifer or Jennifer and Ben or Paris and Nicole suddenly found themselves with more knowable, less remote personalities to root for. Instead of focusing all their attention on those far too privileged to comprehend or relate to, audiences could embrace no-nonsense, surprisingly open-minded Rudy of "Survivor" or despise the outspoken-but-bellicose Susan Hawk. Reality "stars" like lovable couple Chip and Kim from "The Amazing Race" or country-boy Troy from "The Apprentice" offer us a chance to admire real people for qualities that go beyond choosing the perfect dress for the Oscars or smiling sweetly for the cameras.

Plus, now that magazines like *InStyle* make it clear that a major celebrity's image and personality are essentially created by a team of stylists, interior designers, assistants, managers and publicists, it's no wonder we crave an exploration of the little quirks and flaws of ordinary people. And when it comes to making enemies, anyone can throw a temper tantrum and then stalk offstage, but how many ordinary humans can manage the messy explosion of insults and accusations set off by Omarosa of "The Apprentice"? Who knew that "Now *there's* the pot calling the kettle black!" was a racial slur?

Self-Consciousness

Many have argued that self-consciousness will be the death of the genre. As more and more contestants who appear on the shows have been exposed to other reality shows, the argument goes, their actions and statements will become less and less "real." What's to blame here is the popular use of the word "reality" to describe a genre that's never been overtly concerned with realism or even with offering an accurate snapshot of the events featured. In fact, the term "reality TV" may have sprung from "The Real World," in which the "real" was used both in the sense of "the world awaiting young people after they graduate from school," and in the sense of "getting real," or, more specifically, getting all up in someone's grill for eating the last of your peanut butter.

The truth is, part of the entertainment offered by reality TV lies in separating the aspects of subjects' behavior that are motivated by an awareness of the cameras from the aspects that are genuine. You can't expect someone who's surrounded by cameras to act naturally all of the time, and as the genre has evolved, editors and producers have become aware that highlighting this gap between the real self and the camera-ready self not only constitutes quality entertainment, but may be the easiest shortcut to creating the villain character that any provocative narrative requires. When "Big Brother 5's" Jason pouts his lips, flexes his muscles and adjusts his metrosexual headband in the mirror, then confides to the camera that every idiotic thing he's done in the house so far has been part of a master plan to confuse his roommates, he not only makes a great enemy for the more seemingly grounded members of the house, but he also hints at narcissistic and sociopathic streaks that reality TV has demonstrated may be a defining characteristic of the modern personality. Either an alarming number of reality show contestants are self-obsessed and combative, or the common character traits found in young people have shifted dramatically.

In our self-conscious, media-savvy culture, such posturing and preening are a worthy subject for the camera's gaze, documenting as they do the flavor of the times. When young kids talk about marketing themselves properly and "breaking wide," it makes perfect sense to shine a light on the rampant self-consciousness and unrelenting self-involvement of these characters. When we see Puck of "The Real World" screeching at the top of his lungs or Richard Hatch of "Survivor" confiding to the cameras that he considers the other players beneath him, we may be glimpsing behavior that's more true of the average American than any of us would like to believe.

But then, no matter how premeditated many of the words and actions of reality show stars can be, the proper events and tasks eventually conspire to create cracks in the shiny veneer, revealing flaws and personality tics they'd clearly wish to hide. If even the smooth operators of "The Apprentice" stumble on their words, bare their claws and show their less polished selves regularly, you have to figure that keeping your true self hidden from the camera is more difficult than it looks. Katrina, for example, started the first season appearing smooth and polished, then slowly unraveled as the personalities and tactics of the players around her seemed to erode her sense of self. And who can forget Rupert on "Survivor," who went from lovable teddy bear to snarling grizzly whenever someone crossed him? Real people are surprising. The process of getting to know the characters, of discovering the qualities and flaws that define them, and then discussing these discoveries with other viewers creates a simulation of community that most people don't find in their everyday lives. That may be a sad commentary on the way we're living, but it's not the fault of these shows, which unearth a heartfelt desire to make connections with other human beings. Better that we rediscover our interest in other, real people than sink ourselves into the mirage of untouchable celebrity culture or into some überhuman, ultraclever fictional "Friends" universe.

The Power to Amuse and Engage

Naturally, there will always be those shows that heedlessly propagate crass televised stunts without any socially redeeming qualities. "The Swan," which turns normal, attractive women into hideous plasticized demons with lots of pricey plastic surgery, then pits the demons against each other in a beauty contest, is more freakishly dehumanizing than anything [dystopian novelist] George Orwell could've dreamed up. "Gana La Verde," a "Fear Factor"–style competition where immigrants compete for a green card, or at least for the use of lawyers who might win them a green card, makes you wonder if we're not one step away from feeding the underprivileged to the lions on live TV. But the lowest rung on the reality ladder has nothing to do with the sharp, fascinating shows at the top. The best reality shows transform ordinary places and people into dramatic settings populated by lovable heroes and loathsome enemies, and in the process of watching and taking sides and comparing the characters' choices to the ones we might make, we're reacquainted with ourselves and each other. Great fictional TV has the power to engage us, too, but the networks aren't creating much of that these days. When was the last time "CSI" sparked a little self-examination? Does "Still Standing" make you giggle in recognition at life's merry foibles?

Lowbrow or not, all most of us want from TV is the chance to glimpse something true, just a peek at those strange little tics and endearing flaws that make us human. While the networks' safe little formulas mostly seem devoid of such charms, reality shows have the power to amuse, anger, appall, surprise, but most of all, engage us. Isn't that the definition of entertainment?

"If 'reality' programs are a source of
'entertainment' for you and your family,
you must understand one thing: taking
pleasure in the suffering of others is a
form of mental illness called sadism."

Reality TV Fosters Sadism

Michael Goodspeed

Michael Goodspeed argues in the following viewpoint that
reality TV shows are cruel and sadistic. Many of the dire situations they depict have been forecast by science fiction novels written as cautionary tales, Goodspeed contends. In these
novels, he maintains, characters suffer in order to provide entertainment to others, exactly the kind of sadism that charac-
terizes today's reality TV shows. Michael Goodspeed is a radio personality and journalist based in Portland, Oregon.

As you read, consider the following questions:

1. According to the author, Stephen King's book *The
   Running Man* predicted today's reality TV shows. What
   are the similarities and differences between the book and
   reality TV?
2. What are the ethical implications of tricking or scaring
   unsuspecting people for reality TV shows, according to
   Goodspeed?
3. According to the author, what does the popularity of
   reality TV shows suggest about American society?

Michael Goodspeed, "The Cultural Plague of Reality TV," www.rense.com, April
15, 2004. Copyright © 2004 by Rense.com. Reproduced by permission.

The function of science fiction is not always to predict the future but sometimes to prevent it.
                          —Frank Herbert, author of the *Dune* chronicles

Bestselling horror author Stephen King is loath to grant interviews. As he has written in countless forewords of his popular novels, journalists "who should really know better" never fail to ask the most asinine question of all: "Where do you get your ideas?" The question implies that a writer can make withdrawals from the magical "idea bank" when the natural well spring of his imagination runs dry. Actually, that may not be far from the truth. As King himself wrote, ". . . great ideas are not so much invented as discovered."

I've often wondered about the role of the collective unconscious in the creative process. Perhaps this could account for the apparently unintentional ability of some fiction writers to predict the future. The last few years must have King feeling like Nostradamus.

In the late 60's, while King was still in high school, he wrote the shocking novella *Rage*, a story whose protagonist is a psychotic young man who takes his father's gun to school and murders his teachers and principal. After the string of school shootings in the 90's (including two instances when the killers cited King's book as inspiration), King voluntarily took *Rage* out of distribution. On the issue of media influence on youth violence, King once said, "Marilyn Manson and Metallica never caused anyone to kill . . . but these things act as accelerants."

But other early writings of King[1] have proved even more prescient. Two Bachman novellas, *The Long Walk* and *The Running Man*, tell stories of a bleak and once unthinkable future that is unquestionably coming to fruition.

The Long Walk

In the alternative universe of *The Long Walk*, the USA's most celebrated national sport/cultural event/pastime is a grisly endurance event where the participants compete for their very lives. Young men voluntarily sign on for The Long Walk, a race to the death where 100 teenagers begin walking

---

1. King wrote some novels under the fictitious name Richard Bachman.

and do not stop until they get their respective "tickets." Getting a "ticket" results from dropping below the minimum walking speed of four MPH a total of four times in less than one hour. But a "ticket" is not so much a "ticket" as a bullet to the brain. The race continues until one boy is left walking. This lucky young chap will receive a mysterious reward known only as The Prize.

The boys who choose to compete in The Long Walk are celebrated as true "patriots." They are "honored" to be gunned down by rifle-toting Army automatons in front of a national TV audience. The boys cry, plead, clutch cramped legs, and beg for mercy from the placid soldiers . . . all of whom carry out their "orders" with stoic efficiency.

Ratings for The Long Walk, and the resulting advertising revenue, are truly astronomical.

The Running Man

The Running Man tells an equally cruel, though slightly less stomach churning, tale. Its protagonist is Benjamin Richards, an out of work breadwinner for a family of two, unemployed in a barren economy and forced to risk his life on a macabre game show called The Running Man. Richards' task is to elude capture for 30 days from law enforcement and a group of trackers called The Hunters. Citizens are told that Richards is a criminal, and will receive cash rewards as "patriots" if they turn him in. If Richards remains free for 30 days, his prize is a billion dollars. If he gets caught, he gets executed in the most violent manner imaginable on national television.

The world of The Running Man is worse than an Orwellian nightmare.[2] Huge chemical companies (including the aptly named Raygon Chemical) have poisoned the atmosphere so severely that young children are dying of lung cancer. Only the wealthy can afford to breathe healthy air, provided by "nose filters" which run at several thousand dollars a pop (the secret is, nose filters can be made by anyone for a few dollars of cheap material.)

The ending of The Running Man features a chilling synchronism. Richards faces a choice of either joining the evil

2. George Orwell depicts a dystopian totalitarian society in his novel *1984*.

Network which poisons the air and broadcasts *The Running Man* . . . or he can die and take down as many "bad guys" as possible. He hijacks a plane and flies it into the Network's corporate headquarters, the tallest tower in downtown New York. (By the way, if you think I'm implying that the victims of [the September 11, 2001, terrorist attacks] were "bad guys," or that the terrorists were "heroes," think again!)

As recently as 10 years ago, King's scenarios, while undeniably chilling, seemed little more than unmitigated fantasy. Could anyone imagine a world where Americans would stand by and cheer while human beings were slaughtered for sheer entertainment? A recent trend in American media proves that King's speculation was not only plausible, but shockingly fortuitous.

Reality TV

In 2004, the highest rated network television shows are so-called reality programs. This trend began in the late 90's, when CBS brought us the immensely popular *Survivor* series. This show features very attractive people walking around scantily clad on a desert island, nearly starving to death, battling for food and other goodies in inane "competitions" such as eating giant worms and walking on hot coals, and generally conniving, plotting, and scamming one another for the best chance to stay on the show and win a million bucks. Indeed, the "winner" of *Survivor* has often been the biggest jerk who was most adept at forming sinister plots.

Survivor creator Mark Burnett has come under scathing criticism for his latest proposed "reality" program. Burnett has pitched to CBS a show called *Recovery*, which will feature real-life "investigations" and man-hunts into active missing children cases. The people conducting the "hunts" will not be professional law enforcement, but independent bounty hunters and private investigators. CBS' preliminary publicity material describes the show as taking "viewers along on an emotional and life-changing ride, from the abduction to the search in all its intensity to the reunion of child and parents." Child advocacy groups are generally appalled by the concept.

"The idea for Mark Burnett's new reality show of snatching children sickens me," said Lindsey Brooks, investigating manager for Child Quest International in Campbell, Calif. "These children he plans to recover have already been extremely emotionally damaged by being abducted. Now Burnett wants to exploit them by being on a TV show."

Reality TV Distracts Americans from Their Nation's Moral Decay

It is the reality behind reality shows that serves to mask the whittling away of basic constitutional rights and freedoms. Instead of circuses and Christians being martyred by lions in public arenas in order to distract the people from the implosion of the Roman Empire, the people of the United States are being bombarded with shows that turn us into opportunistic voyeurs bereft of any sense of morality, compassion or common decency. Slowly, our sense of outrage is anesthetized.

Diana L. Hayes, *National Catholic Reporter*, June 20, 2003.

At least *Recovery* would have the redeeming value of attempting to save real children. Other "reality" shows have plumbed the depths of mankind's potential for sadism and cruelty. The "entertainment" of these shows is provided by the physical, emotional, and spiritual anguish of its participants, many of whom are 100% non-consenting.

The highest rated television show in the USA is *American Idol*, a "talent" competition for aspiring young dancers and singers. The real "entertainment" of the show is provided by judge Simon Cowell, who verbally disembowels the show's participants with allegedly "humorous" insults. Heavy metal artist Ozzy Osbourne had this to stay about the viciously acerbic Cowell: "I'd like to see that . . . guy have a go at it, see how it feels."

Bad Taste

Other Fox reality shows have not only pushed but torn through the envelope of bad taste. *Joe Millionaire* featured vapid young women competing to "win" a million dollars by being chosen as the bride of a super rich guy. The joke was, he was completely broke!

Another Fox show, *My Big Fat Obnoxious Fiance*, featured an even more sadistic premise. A beautiful young woman is told she can split a million bucks with a fat, repulsive man if they both convince their families they are engaged to be married. The joke is, the guy is an actor, so the real object of ridicule is the greedy, blushing bride. The young woman may be held accountable for her own vacuity, but the woman's family were unwitting and non-consenting victims. The show's "entertainment" was the tearful, horrified, grief-stricken reactions of her siblings and parents to the "fat, obnoxious fiance." MBFOF's crescendo, a desperate confession by the make-believe couple, was one of the most discomfiting displays in the history of television. The young woman blubbered her apologies to her shell-shocked family, begging their forgiveness for the despicable sham.

Fox's capacity for repugnant exploitation is apparently without limit. The latest Fox reality show, called *The Swan*, offers free plastic surgery to "homely" women in an attempt to make them "beautiful." The "most beautiful" of the mutilated women will compete in a beauty pagent in the show's climax. But as we hear in the trailer for this Fox gem, ". . . not everyone will be good enough to make the cut."

Cruelty

But even more disturbingly, some new reality shows not only push and cross the bounds of good taste, but actually physically endanger their unwitting, non-consenting "participants." On the Sci-Fi channel's *Scare Tactics*, individuals are set up by their "friends" for extraordinarily ghoulish and realistic pranks. The majority of these victims are actually led to believe their lives are in danger. In one episode, a group of friends in a car pick up a mysterious hitchhiker, only to see him turn violent and attack the driver with a knife. Not surprisingly, the "mark" in the back seat, believing his friend is being murdered, pummels the poor actor with a knife into submission. Another *Scare Tactics* prank went even more terribly wrong, and has resulted in litigation. A Los Angeles woman named Kara Blanc sued the cable channel for "severe emotional damage and injuries incurred as a result," after a prank in which Blanc ran naked through a desert canyon, believing she was being chased by aliens who had murdered her friends.

Season 3 of *Scare Tactics* has featured the most vicious pranks to date. In Epsiode 2, a group of young men out for a joy ride get pulled over by the "cops." The young "mark" witnesses one of his friends (an accomplice) flee from the "police," only to be shot in the back by a remorseless officer. The "mark" says tearfully to the cop, "I can't believe you just shot that kid!" The officer then directs the young man to "turn his back," to which the boy replies, "You're gonna shoot me, aren't you?" The officer then trains his gun directly on the boy and says, "I'm gonna do what I have to do." But never fear, young man! Seconds later, he was given the delightful news, "You're on *Scare Tactics!*" Har-de-har-har, indeed. . . .

Predictably, some moronic and highly impressionable people have tried to imitate the antics seen on *Scare Tactics* in real life. In Ohio in October of 2003, a young woman set up her "best friend" to be kidnapped by two men and dragged into a field at gunpoint. The men proceeded to "murder" their female accomplice, then held a gun to the victim's head . . . and began counting down. After reaching "one," they yelled out, "Happy Halloween! You're on *Scare Tactics!*" Not surprisingly, neither the victim nor Ohio authorities were amused by this horrific prank, and the perpetrators, if convicted, will face one to five years behind bars.

It is understandable why so many networks are seeking to profit from the hugely popular reality craze. With no actors, directors, or writers to pay, these shows have ridiculously low production costs, almost always turning an enormous profit. Reality shows are a source of frequent "water cooler discussions," and are even the subject of "reports" on many network newscasts. Even if you don't watch these shows, you can keep abreast of "story" developments by tuning in to Tom Brokaw or Dan Rather on a nightly basis.

Turn Off the TV

If "reality" programs are a source of "entertainment" for you and your family, you must understand one thing: taking pleasure in the suffering of others is a form of mental illness called sadism. Watch these shows if you like, but as you guffaw at the sight of innocent, unwilling, non-consenting humans suffering enormous mental and physical anguish, take a moment to look in the mirror, and ask yourself if you like what you see.

Recent Hollywood films *Gladiator* and *The Passion of the Christ* have shed light on the extraordinary cruelty of the Roman Empire. Public torture, execution, and sacrifice of human beings was the preferred form of entertainment for the Romans. Many have compared current trends in American culture to the last days just before Rome fell. Some even say that no culture in the history of the world has ever recovered from the depth of decay we are currently experiencing in American society.

Saturday, April 17th [2004], marks the beginning of National Turn Your TV Off Week in my hometown of Portland, OR. Far be it from me to tell anyone how to spend their free time, but might I suggest that you use this week as an opportunity to tune off your TV, and tune in to the greatest reality show of all, called real life.

> "*Art tells us who we are and what we are capable of. Unfortunately, [the video game Grand Theft Auto] does this well, which is what I think scares us.*"

Violent Video Games Can Promote an Understanding of Human Nature

Thom Gillespie

In the following viewpoint Thom Gillespie contends that *Grand Theft Auto* (*GTA*) is the latest video game to be accused of corrupting America's youth. However, video games such as *GTA* are art and deserve protection, he claims. Moreover, such games merely reflect humanity's violent impulses; they do not incite violence, Gillespie argues. These games also offer opportunities for debates about ethical issues and the consequences of actions. Thom Gillespie is a professor of telecommunications and director of the Masters in Immersive Mediated Environments program at Indiana University in Bloomington.

As you read, consider the following questions:

1. According to the author, why are young people today more likely to be playing video games such as *Grand Theft Auto* than watching television or movies?
2. Why does the author believe that violent video games such as *Grand Theft Auto* should be protected?
3. How is the author's experience with Father Kaiser's programs similar, in his opinion, to video games such as *GTA*?

Thom Gillespie, "*Grand Theft Auto*, the Video Game Everyone Loves to Hate, Allows Ethics and Morality Lessons," *Technos Quarterly*, vol. 11, Winter 2002. Copyright © 2002 by the Agency for Instructional Technology. Reproduced by permission.

"Grand Theft Auto III takes place in Liberty City—a completely unique universe with its own laws, standards, ethics, and morals (or lack thereof). There are dozens of ways to take out the inhabitants: punches, kicks, head butts, baseball bats, handguns, Uzis, AK-47s, shotguns, M-16s, sniper rifles, rocket launchers, grenades, Molotov cocktails, and flame throwers. . . . Let the crime wave begin!"

—from page 4 of *Grand Theft Auto III Official Strategy Guide*

Sound like fun? Your kids think this video game is a blast. You might, too, if you considered the teaching opportunities it presents.

If you haven't heard about Grand Theft Auto, let me tell you about it. GTA, as it's affectionately known by its users, is the latest thing to send our kids and society in general to hell in a handbasket. We have been warned about watching out for everything from the written word, to the novel, to film, to comics, to rock music, TV, rap music, the Internet, and a steady stream of video games which are corrupting minds and morals at an ever-increasing pace. Before it was Doom and Quake; now it is GTA. I beg to differ.

I teach game design at Indiana University in the MIME [Masters in Immersive Mediated Environments] program, so I actually "have" to study games. I have a research budget, some of which I use to buy Play Stations and lots of games. I also buy strategy guides because these games are in reality too difficult for a guy with a Ph.D. in information science from the University of California at Berkeley to figure out in a normal time frame, like say, a school term. This term I have been spending a lot of time trying to understand how GTA is corrupting minds and morals. I haven't figured out the minds-and-morals thing yet, but I have discovered that there are some amazing areas where using GTA in my university classroom with the students is a wildly enlightening experience for both myself and the kids.

GTA: A Wonderful Tool for Teaching Ethics and Morality

The most recent edition of GTA, Vice, sold close to 1.4 million units in two days at 50 dollars a pop, which means two things: 1) this is a really big industry, and 2) most of the kids I normally meet in a classroom are more likely to have played GTA than they are to have watched *The Sopranos* or *Buffy* [*the Vampire Slayer*] on TV. Like rock music in the '60s and '70s, the game industry is driving culture at the moment.

Because so many kids have played GTA, it is really easy to get a runaway conversation going in class with little prompting from me other than a question such as: "So, what do you think of GTA?"

Remember, I teach game designers, so what they don't reply with is "cool"—no matter how you spell the word. The usual response is that the game is terrible in a moral sense. And, then the class explodes in amazing directions.

Some folks will point out that the alleged violence is virtual and not real and probably a great improvement on spectator violence of the past, such as picnic outings to witness hangings, stonings, beheadings, various battles during the Civil War in the United States, and crucifixions, which were actually a regular occurrence in the days of Christ. And someone usually points out that the Coliseum, that great tourist destination in Rome, was the sight of regular real mayhem witnessed and cheered for by many. So, maybe the virtual violence of GTA and Doom and Quake serves a survival need in human beings. Maybe this thirst for blood is slaked by the game. This sort of discussion tends to bring a moment of reflection—and then inevitably someone will launch into the whole aspect of censorship.

The students look at GTA and other games and talk about violence in the *Last Exit to Brooklyn*, the Dutch film *The Vanishing*, *Hamlet*, *King Lear*, *Othello*, and *Rashomon*, where evil and lies succeed and thrive just as they do in the real world. The discussion moves to the difference that GTA is a game, and therefore the audience disappears and the interactor appears—and this makes us all nervous: pseudo consequential decision making. After all, GTA is a game where you play within a crime wave, most of which you are creating.

Art, Not Reality

Then the discussion hones onto the real hot-button issue of GTA, the fact that you can hire a prostitute to have sex with you—depicted by a rocking car you have entered—and after the deed has been done, you can kill the prostitute and take her money. This is obviously a really bad thing to do, and as far as I can determine, none of my students has gone out and actually done such a thing in real life, but just the idea of such an event mortifies most.

Doing Harmful Things in a Harmless Context

It is essential to remember that this adventure is taking place on a big-screen television and not downtown. It is essential to remember that no child has beaten up a police officer, had sex with a prostitute or done drugs when the game is over. They're simply playing with the idea of doing harmful things in a harmless context.

So as we think about Grand Theft Auto III and in general about much media aimed at children, I say to you: Lighten up. Think a bit about why pretending to do bad things is fun. And be grateful if the bad things children do are contained by a flickering, flat screen.

Crispin Sartwell, *Atlanta Journal-Constitution*, January 9, 2002.

The discussion will wander on . . . and then someone brings up the fact that as far as anyone can determine, this specific action was not hard wired into the game but may be an emergent action which combines two rules of Liberty City: you can have sex with prostitutes, and you can kill and rob anyone in Liberty City. Therefore, after having sex with a prostitute, you can kill and rob her and get your money back. The idea of this action freezes most students no matter what the discussion, but they do note that in context of the logic of Liberty City—with "its own laws, standards, ethics, and morals (or lack thereof)"—it makes sense. You are in a crime wave; anyone in Liberty City can be robbed, beaten, or killed; cars can be hijacked and crashed into walls or people. But if you hit someone, you will be hit back. If you hit a streetwalker, she will hit you back, and if you are in the Red Light district, all the streetwalkers will gang up on you until you run away or they kill you. If you crash a car into enough objects or overturn the car, it will explode and your character will die. There is a definite consequence to actions in GTA. . . .

I don't worry about this too much simply because of media-effects research, which basically says that media can increase the probability that someone does something they are inclined to do but has almost no ability to make most folks do something they are not inclined to do.

It's Art, After All

Eventually the discussion always comes to the big point. GTA is art, like it or not—it may or may not be great art; only time determines this. But, it needs the same protection and respect as DuChamp's Urinal, Picasso's Guernica, Serrano's Piss Christ, and the Garbage Pail Kid cards. Years ago there was a fad called the Garbage Pail Kid cards which were disgusting gross-out cards aimed at little boys who loved disgusting gross-outs. The odd thing about the Garbage Pail Kids was that the idea was developed by Art Spiegelman, a comic book artist who eventually went on to take his disgusting talent and give us *Maus*, the retelling of the Holocaust with comic versions of cats and mice. *Maus* won a Pulitzer prize. We can't have it both ways. We can't protect only some speech and some words and some images and some games. Art tells us who we are and what we are capable of. Unfortunately, GTA does this well, which is what I think scares us.

GTA seems to encourage my students to consider why the game is successful as a game, and it also forces them to make decisions as to whether they would spend time building something like GTA. This is what teaching is all about. I can't get this discussion out of Pajama Sam, I can't get this discussion out of Rockett, I can't get this discussion out of the Sims or Black & White. I can get this discussion out of GTA. For that I am thankful.

Scared Straight?

Thinking about GTA and my students making decisions as players and designers working in the world caused me to think back to grade school decades ago. I went to Catholic school in Philadelphia. My teachers were nuns, and for the most part they were obsessed with the sins we might commit. The consensus seemed to be that they could scare us into being good. Promising us an eternity of fire and brimstone worked pretty well until about sixth grade, at which time the hormones kicked in and some things seemed worth the risk (mostly anything having to do with sex). I guess the nuns knew we had passed to another level, so at that point, they brought out the heavy hitter: Father Ellwood E. Kieser.

Father Kieser founded Paulist Productions in 1968 to produce life-enriching programming and preach the gospel. Father Kieser created a weekly anthology series called *Insight*, which the nuns showed us every Friday around 2:30 P.M., just before school got out for the weekend. I think they thought of *Insight* as a potential weekend inoculation against sin. For me, I waited for *Insight* every week. It was the highlight of my week. It was excellent television with a message, but the message never seemed too heavy-handed and Father Kieser never seemed to tell me what to think so much as to suggest points of view. Watching *Insight* made me feel as if I had a choice in decisions that would affect my future.

I can imagine a Father Kieser in the world today. I imagine that he would look on GTA and see possibilities to produce life-enriching programming and preach the gospel in ways never imagined by creating consequential situations where choices are made which are fun, ethical, and moral. I have no illusion that any of the folks who designed GTA gave much thought to real morality—but I don't think they should have. They created a fun, tightly modeled world in which kids love to play.

I think it is important that folks who work with kids understand the games which are attractive to them and why they are attractive to them so that they can use these games in ways Father Kieser might have done for similar impact. GTA is rated an adult game just as many movies are rated as adult material. We know kids see adult movies, and we know kids play adult games. It is part of a kid becoming an adult, trying to jump the turnstile as early as possible; we have all done it. I work with adults, so I can bring the games into my classrooms and not get into trouble—but most of you cannot do this (otherwise, I'd be reading about you in *USA Today*). I think it is reasonable to talk about the media your kids are playing with. They want to talk about their media, and they can talk deeply about this media and what it means to them.

This is important. As they get older the next level of discussion is when they start to design and build, and the discussion will then turn to what they as human beings, as artists, want to bring into the world and leave for their children. The potential is there—but only if you, the teacher, are willing to play and learn. Can't just criticize the book jacket.

> "A communication system is totally neutral. It has no conscience, no principle, no morality. It has only a history. It will broadcast filth or inspiration with equal facility. It will speak the truth as lightly as it will speak falsehood. It is, in sum, no more, no less than the men and women who use it."
>
> —Edward R. Murrow of CBS Broadcasting

"The heads of six major health-care organizations testified jointly before Congress in June 2000 that there is a direct causal link between violent video games and violence."

Violent Video Games Promote Violence

Jack Thompson

According to Jack Thompson in the following viewpoint, the obsessive playing of violent video games by young people can lead directly to real violence. He claims that the fact that the Department of Defense uses the same video games to train soldiers to kill as consumers buy proves that such games desensitize players to violence. He argues that there have been numerous cases of teen violence committed by obsessive players of violent video games. Jack Thompson is a Miami-based attorney and activist.

As you read, consider the following questions:
1. According to the author, why do violent video games have a greater impact on teens than they do on adults?
2. What activities do players of *Grand Theft Auto III* engage in, as described by Thompson?
3. How should parents combat the influence of violent video games, in the author's opinion?

Jack Thompson, "Video Games Train Young Killers," *Beacon (Ohio) Journal*, October 6, 2003. Copyright © 2003 by *Beacon Journal* and wire services. All rights reserved. Reproduced by permission of the author.

A teen-age boy, Dustin Lynch, will be tried for murder in a courtroom in Medina County. The adults who trained him to kill will not be mentioned at the trial, but they should be.

In April 1999, I appeared on NBC's *Today* show with the parents of three Paducah, Ky., girls who had been shot and killed by a teen trained on the violent video game *Doom*. We predicted that other teen-age boys in other high schools would do likewise.

Eight days later, Dylan Klebold and Eric Harris gave us the school massacre in suburban Denver known as "Columbine." These boys had trained for months on *Doom*, an interactive murder simulator that makes killing fun, efficient and remorseless.

Defense Department Games

Our own U.S. Defense Department has set up the Institute for Creative Technologies at the University of Southern California. The institute takes your taxpayer dollars and hires video game industry software geniuses to design its killing simulation "games," which are used to desensitize teen recruits to acts of violence to get them, in combat, to kill.

The industry then distributes the same games to teen civilians.

Why should it surprise that games that have a desensitizing effect on teen soldiers have the same effect on teen civilians?

The heads of six major health-care organizations testified jointly before Congress in June 2000 that there is a direct causal link between violent video games and violence. Various medical research facilities, including Harvard, have found that teens process violent images in a different part of the brain than do adults, the part that is unable to differentiate reality from fantasy and that, according to Harvard, makes copycatting far more likely in kids than in adults.

A study conducted at Indiana University proves the games actually cause brain damage in kids at the cellular level.

Obsessive Gamers

I have a sworn statement of a Medina man who was with Dustin Lynch when he obsessively played *Grand Theft Auto*

III for hours at a time. This is a game in which you steal cars, kill police officers, have sex with a prostitute and then kill her to get your money back.

This witness says, under oath, that Lynch's favorite way to kill in the game was to "beat victims with a baseball bat because you get more points for killing at close range."

Cardow. © 2003 by Cagle Cartoons, Inc. Reproduced by permission.

This witness also swears that Lynch said it was the only game he ever played and that he was incredibly proficient at winning the game as the killer. The witness called Lynch "zombified" when he played the game.

A recent Gallup Poll found that 71 percent of all teen-age boys have played the *Grand Theft Auto* games, and Gallup found that they are twice as likely to engage in acts of violence than those who have not played that game.

Eleven days ago [September 24, 2003], a Cold Spring, Minn., 15-year-old boy shot two fellow students, killing one and critically wounding another. Guess what video game he obsessively played, according to neighbors with whom I have spoken? *Grand Theft Auto: Vice City.*

There are numerous other murders directly tied by the police to this one game, but space does not allow their recounting.

To all . . . parents, I say: Look at all your kids' video games. If any appear to be violent in content, throw them out, or, better yet, take them back to the store and demand your money back.

And then, having done all that, hold onto your kids and keep them away, as best you can, from kids who obsessively play killing games. A tragedy could happen to you as well.

Think not? Talk to Medina's lonely father, Mickey Mishne, whose 17-year-old daughter, JoLynn, Dustin is accused of killing.

"Hip-Hop for many young people is the proclamation that they are independent and intolerant of much of what they consider to be adult society, which they frequently view as hypocritical."

Rap Music Provides a Realistic View of Life

Carl S. Taylor and Virgil Taylor

Hip-hop culture and the rap music at its core are enormously influential, claim Carl S. Taylor and Virgil Taylor in the following viewpoint. Like rock-and-roll music before it, rap was originally rejected by mainstream adult culture, and this rejection only strengthened it, Taylor and Taylor maintain. They assert that the appeal of rap music to young people is its expression of a more honest view of life than the one adults offer. Carl S. Taylor is the editor of the *Journal of Urban Youth Culture*.

As you read, consider the following questions:
1. According to Taylor and Taylor, what are some of the components of early rap music?
2. In the authors' view, what is the appeal of rap music to white youth?
3. What is the hip-hop view of life, according to the authors?

Carl S. Taylor and Virgil Taylor, "Hip-Hop and Youth Culture: Contemplations on an Emerging Cultural Phenomenon," www.juyc.org, January 2004. Copyright © 2004 by the *Journal of Urban Youth Culture*. Reproduced by permission.

Throughout the last twenty-five years, a new form of expression has continued to evolve despite the efforts of many in the so-called "establishment" to minimize its influence on young people. Hip-Hop, once limited to urban music and dance has become a widespread form of communication exhibited and enjoyed by young people throughout the world. Hip-Hop is no longer limited to rap music and break dancing; today it represents a multi-billion dollar industry that influences everything from automotive design and fashion to primetime television programming, collegiate and professional sports, mass media marketing and Madison Avenue advertising. Today Hip-Hop is for many a way of life, a culture that is intricately woven into every aspect of young people's daily lives.

In contemplating this phenomenon and making an effort to understand not only its foundation but the premise that comprises the root of Hip-Hop ideology, it is important to remember that this emerging culture has similarities to other cultures that have emerged throughout history. Hip-Hop was initially born of the ability of those early practitioners of rap music, DJ wizardry and street-corner fashion creation to overcome their inability to gain acceptance and recognition by the established music, fashion and entertainment industries.

Further galvanizing the fledgling culture was the lack of acceptance by adult culture, who refused to recognize these newly emerging forms of expression as legitimate. This was particularly true where many parents were concerned. Needless to say, if parents and other authority figures didn't understand Hip-Hop, didn't like it and, in many instances, admonished young people for embracing it, young people were even more compelled to further immerse themselves in this newly developing culture.

A Complex System of Ideas, Values, and Concepts

Hip-Hop, like Rock 'n' Roll before it, is not only a genre of music, but also a complex system of ideas, values and concepts that reflect newly emerging and ever-changing creative correlative expressive mechanisms including but not limited to song, poetry, film and fashion. In the early days, Hip-Hop was primarily related to the rhyming, rhythmic spoken word art-form known as rapping. Rapping is, in fact, not a new method of creative expression. The ease with which young people can participate in this form of creativity seems to have helped the phenomenal growth of this genre of music and expression.

Review of rap music lyrics and styling from the early to mid-1970's, when Hip-Hop began, reveals several aspects of the musical genre that appear to have had significant appeal to young people, particularly those in urban communities. There has never been one all-inclusive form of rap music. It covers a broad range of ideas, styling and techniques that are unique to specific demographic areas, geographic regions and territories and locales. The following comprises some of the hallmarks of early rap music:

- Simple yet dominant percussive patterns.
- Limited reliance on traditional musical systems of chord, verse, chorus and other formal and/or traditional methods of Western musical structure.
- Non-traditional utilization of musical instruments including the human voice; i.e., the technique known as "beat boxing" where a person imitates the sounds of percussive instruments. Another Hip-Hop innovation is the technique utilized by the DJ (acronym for disc jockey) known as scratching. Scratching is when DJs rhythmically drag the turntable stylus across a record, so that the needle creates unique "scratching" sounds. Over the years, it has become an art-form.
- Rapping serves as a method of declaring pride in one's community. It also becomes a form of competition whereby a rapper can display his skills and defend his neighborhood or community. This competition was created during the early days of rap, commonly referred to as "battling."
- Early rap relied heavily on lyrical compositions that expressed the joy of immersing oneself in the music, dancing, partying and competing in the various forms of musical expression particularly rapping, scratching and break-dancing.
- Spontaneous "rapping" (delivery of rhythmic lyrical compositions) known as "free styling" comprised many com-

petitions between rappers from school corridors and grounds to streetcorners to large promoted demonstrations. Competitions have remained a mainstay of Hip-Hop culture.

It is interesting to note that rap music was widely ignored by the music industry until approximately the mid-1980's. Even the ground-breaking, innovative cable television music program MTV stayed clear of rap music and Hip-Hop during its infancy. It was when rap music became more violent and volatile that the music industry became interested in the possibilities the genre represented, at least from a business perspective.

The Appeal of Rap Music

Part of the appeal of rap music appears to be its ability to easily deliver the message of the author or the artist to the listener. Much like blues and country music, Hip-Hop is a form of music that is close to the hearts of many of its listeners. Rap lyrics echo familiar themes that [listeners] can identify with, including young people involved in gang culture.

There are many who question why Hip-Hop culture appeals to young people who have no association with urban communities or urban culture. There is no clear-cut answer to this question, but it would appear that the fascination with urban culture for many middle- and upper-middle-class young people is nothing new. During Prohibition, it was typical for young affluent white youth to frequent the "juke joints" and taverns of urban communities. Other forms of music throughout history have attracted those young people that were prohibited from listening to music that was not part of their respective culture and therefore was not culturally acceptable.

A Separate Culture

The advent of television changed how young people are influenced and, as global communications become faster and more far-reaching, new cultures are more readily revealed and promulgated. Hip-Hop for many young people is the proclamation that they are independent and intolerant of much of what they consider to be adult society, which they frequently view as hypocritical. Whereas conventional wisdom states that family, school, church and community are the primary influences on young people, Hip-Hop declares otherwise.

Part of a Rich Black Tradition

Rap music belongs to a rich Black tradition of reverence for rhetoric in its written and spoken form. Thus, discussions surrounding rap music must see this art form as part of the Black rhetorical continuum, both borrowing from and expanding this tradition in its creative use of language and rhetorical styles and strategies. Most specifically, rap was created and continues to exist primarily as a young, African American (predominantly male) rhetoric of resistance primarily to issues of race. Though rap artists' approaches differ to these issues, as an art form rap music uniformly draws on and expands the Black rhetorical tradition.

Baruti N. Kopano, *Western Journal of Black Studies*, Winter 2002.

Hip-Hop is having a profound affect on young people throughout the world, as technology spreads the gospel of this new way of thinking and the ideology is reinforced in the things young people are exposed to daily. Hip-Hop is not a monolithic voice or idea but rather a complex hybrid of democratic values, street culture ideology, prison culture philosophy, rock 'n' roll, rhythm and blues, jazz, world music and reggae doctrine, and African American and Latino American creeds and cultural traits and so on and so on.

In recent years, Hip-Hop has become the voice for many angry young white males who have chosen to dispel many of the myths that being young and white in America allows easy attainment of the American dream. Marshall Mathers, a young white man from the Detroit, Michigan, area has skyrocketed to fame as Eminem, by providing a dark view of his world, a view apparently shared by many young white men throughout America.

The Hip-Hop View of Life

Polls conducted throughout the United States and parts of Europe reveal that many young people are drawn to Hip-Hop because not only is it exciting to them, but it provides them with a brutally honest view of life. As one young man responded when asked why he liked Hip-Hop, "Because it's real, man. It ain't fake like all that shit the government and everybody be putting down." When asked to elaborate, this young man went on to explain.

"Look at the war in Iraq, man, where the weapons they said was there, how come gas prices went up when all that oil is over there? Look at how the vice-president was hooked up with the companies that got paid over there. Man, they must think people real stupid. And then look at the priests in the Catholic Church, playing with li'l boys and shit. Everybody talk about Eminem and cats in Hip-Hop, but at least they real with theirs, and that's how I'm living, being real and trying to get paid."

Being Real

This view is indicative of the mindset of many in Hip-Hop culture. Whether subscribing to the ideology of being "gangsta" or simply being radical in their thinking and views of the world, the shared theme throughout Hip-Hop is being "real." It is perhaps in this "being real" that the culture finds its willingness to be arrogant and unapologetic in its brazen disregard for anyone that does not appreciate what Hip-Hop is. Therein also lies some of the confusion, because there is as stated earlier no one consistent theme regarding what Hip-Hop is.

From the "bling-bling" of such Hip-Hop artists as 50 Cent, to the gritty southern Nappy Roots, from the macabre theater of the Insane Clown Posse to the pimpish styling of Snoop Dogg. The themes are as broad and conflicted as the frequent disagreements and altercations that arise between various camps in Hip-Hop.

"The attitude and style expressed in the hip-hop 'identity' keeps blacks down."

Rap Music Harms the Black Community

John McWhorter

In the following viewpoint John McWhorter argues that gangsta rap focuses on all of the worst problems of the inner city: drugs, prostitution, and gang violence. In addition, many rap lyrics are degrading to women, he asserts. According to McWhorter, some defenders of rap music suggest that it serves as the voice of unempowered black youth. In reality, however, rap music is harmful to the black community because it links it to racism, violence, and misogyny. John McWhorter, a senior fellow in public policy at the Manhattan Institute, studies various aspects of race and ethnicity.

As you read, consider the following questions:

1. According to the author, how is rap music influencing young black men's behavior?
2. According to McWhorter, what crimes has rapper Sean "P. Diddy" Combs committed?
3. Why does McWhorter believe that many rap musicians are hypocrites?

John McWhorter, "Rap Only Ruins," *New York Post*, August 10, 2003. Copyright © 2002 by *New York Post*. Reproduced by permission.

Not long ago, I was having lunch in a KFC in Harlem, sitting near eight African-American boys, aged about 14. They were extremely loud and unruly, tossing food at one another and leaving it on the floor.

What struck me most was how fully the boys' music—hard-edged rap, preaching bone-deep dislike of authority—provided them with a continuing soundtrack to their anti-social behavior. So completely was rap ingrained in their consciousness that every so often, one or another of them would break into cocky, expletive-laden rap lyrics, accompanied by the angular, bellicose gestures typical of rap performance. A couple of his buddies would then join him. Rap was a running decoration in their conversation.

Many writers and thinkers see a kind of informed political engagement, even a revolutionary potential, in rap and hip-hop. They couldn't be more wrong. By reinforcing the stereotypes that long hindered blacks, and by teaching young blacks that a thuggish adversarial stance is the properly "authentic" response to a presumptively racist society, rap retards black success.

Early rap began not as a growl from below but as happy party music. The first big rap hit, the Sugar Hill Gang's 1978 "Rapper's Delight," featured a catchy bass groove that drove the music forward, as the jolly rapper celebrated himself as a ladies' man and a great dancer.

A string of ebullient raps ensued in the months ahead. At the time, I assumed it was a harmless craze, certain to run out of steam soon.

The "Gangsta" Style

But rap took a dark turn in the early 1980s, as this "bubble gum" music gave way to a "gangsta" style that picked up where blaxploitation left off. Now top rappers began to write edgy lyrics celebrating street warfare or drugs and promiscuity. Grandmaster Flash's ominous 1982 hit, "The Message," with its chorus, "It's like a jungle sometimes, it makes me wonder how I keep from going under," marked the change in sensibility. It depicted ghetto life as profoundly desolate:

You grow in the ghetto, living second Rate/And your eyes will sing a song of deep hate.

> *The places you play and where you stay*
> *Looks like one great big alley way.*
> *You'll admire all the numberbook takers,/Thugs, pimps and*
> *pushers, and the big money makers.*

Music critics fell over themselves to praise "The Message," treating it as the poetry of the streets—as the elite media has characterized hip-hop ever since. The ultimate message of "The Message"—that ghetto life is so hopeless that an explosion of violence is both justified and imminent—would become a hip-hop mantra in the years ahead.

The angry, oppositional stance that "The Message" reintroduced into black popular culture transformed rap from a fad into a multi-billion-dollar industry that sold more than 80 million records in the U.S. in 2002—nearly 13 percent of all recordings sold. To rap producers like Russell Simmons, earlier black pop was just sissy music. He despised the "soft, unaggressive music (and non-threatening images)" of artists like Michael Jackson or Luther Vandross. "So the first chance I got," he says, "I did exactly the opposite."

In the two decades since "The Message," hip-hop performers have churned out countless rap numbers that celebrate a ghetto life of unending violence and criminality.

Police forces became marauding invaders in the gangsta-rap imagination. The late West Coast rapper Tupac Shakur expressed the attitude:

> *Ya gotta know how to shake the snakes, Nigga/'Cause the police love*
> *to break a Nigga/Send him upstate 'cause they straight up hate the*
> *nigga.*

Shakur's anti-police tirade seems tame, however, compared with Ice-T's infamous "Cop Killer":

> *I got my 12-gauge sawed-off.*
> *I got my headlights turned off.*
> *I'm 'bout to bust some shots off.*
> *I'm 'bout to dust some cops off. . . .*

Disrespecting Women

Rap also began to offer some of the most icily misogynistic music human history has ever known.

Here's Schooly D:

> *Tell you now, brother, this ain't no joke,*

She got me to the crib, she laid me on the bed,/I f—d her from my toes to the top of my head./I finally realized the girl was a whore,/ Gave her ten dollars, she asked me for some more.

As N.W.A. (an abbreviation of "Niggers with Attitude") tersely sums up the hip-hop worldview: "Life ain't nothin' but bitches and money."

Hip-hop exploded into popular consciousness at the same time as the music video, and rappers were soon all over MTV, reinforcing in images the ugly world portrayed in rap lyrics. Video after video features rap stars flashing jewelry, driving souped-up cars, sporting weapons, angrily gesticulating at the camera and cavorting with interchangeable, mindlessly gyrating, scantily clad women.

The Nastiest Rap Sells Best

Of course, not all hip-hop is belligerent or profane—entire CDs of gang-bangin', police-baiting, woman-bashing invective would get old fast to most listeners. But it's the nastiest rap that sells best, and the nastiest cuts that make a career. As I write, the top 10 best-selling hip-hop recordings are 50 Cent (currently with the second-best-selling record in the nation among all musical genres), Bone Crusher, Lil' Kim, Fabolous, Lil' Jon and the East Side Boyz, Cam'ron Presents the Diplomats, Busta Rhymes, Scarface, Mobb Deep and Eminem.

Every one of these groups or performers personifies willful opposition to society and every one celebrates the ghetto as "where it's at." Thus, the occasional dutiful songs in which a rapper urges men to take responsibility for their kids or laments senseless violence are mere garnish. Keeping the thug front and center has become the quickest and most likely way to become a star.

No hip-hop luminary has worked harder than Sean "P. Diddy" Combs, the wildly successful rapper, producer, fashion mogul and CEO of Bad Boy Records, to cultivate a gangsta image. Combs may have grown up middle-class in Mount Vernon, New York, and even have attended Howard University for a while, but he's proven he can gang-bang with the worst. Cops charged Combs with possession of a deadly weapon in 1995. In 1999, he faced charges for assaulting a rival record executive.

Most notoriously, police charged him that year with firing a gun at a nightclub in response to an insult, injuring three bystanders and with fleeing the scene with his entourage (including then-pal Jennifer Lopez).

The Grim Rapper

'GANGSTA' MUSIC

Margulies. © 1997 by *The New Jersey Record*. Reproduced by permission of Jimmy Margulies.

Combs and his crew are far from alone among rappers in keeping up the connection between "rap and rap sheet," as critic Kelefa Sanneh artfully puts it. Several prominent rappers, including superstar Tupac Shakur, have gone down in hails of bullets—with other rappers often suspected in the killings. Death Row Records producer Marion "Suge" Knight just finished a five-year prison sentence for assault and federal weapons violations.

Rap's Misguided Defenders

Many fans, rappers, producers and intellectuals defend hiphop's violence, both real and imagined, and its misogyny as a revolutionary cry of frustration from disempowered youth. For Simmons, gangsta raps "teach listeners something about the lives of the people who create them and remind them that these people exist." 50 Cent recently told *Vibe* magazine, "Mainstream America can look at me and say, 'That's the mentality of a young man from the 'hood.'"

University of Pennsylvania black studies professor Michael Eric Dyson has written a book-length paean to Shakur, praising him for "challenging narrow artistic visions of black identity" and for "artistically exploring the attractions and limits of black moral and social subcultures"—just one of countless fawning treatises on rap published in recent years.

But we're sorely lacking in imagination if in 2003—long after the civil rights revolution proved a success, at a time of vaulting opportunity for African Americans, when blacks find themselves at the top reaches of society and politics—we think that it signals progress when black kids rattle off violent, sexist, nihilistic lyrics, like Russians reciting Pushkin.

How is it progressive to describe life as nothing but "bitches and money"? Or to tell impressionable black kids, who'd find every door open to them if they just worked hard and learned, that blowing a rival's head off is "real"? How helpful is rap's sexism in a community plagued by rampant illegitimacy and an excruciatingly low marriage rate?

The idea that rap is an authentic cry against oppression is all the sillier when you recall that black Americans had lots more to be frustrated about in the past but never produced or enjoyed music as nihilistic as 50 Cent or N.W.A. On the contrary, black popular music was almost always affirmative and hopeful.

Harmful to the Black Community

OK, maybe rap isn't progressive in any meaningful sense, some observers will admit; but isn't it just a bunch of kids blowing off steam and so nothing to worry about? I think that response is too easy. With music videos, DVD players, Walkmans, the Internet, clothes and magazines all making hip-hop an accompaniment to a person's entire existence, we need to take it more seriously. In fact, I would argue that it is seriously harmful to the black community.

The attitude and style expressed in the hip-hop "identity" keeps blacks down. Almost all hip-hop, gangsta or not, is delivered with a cocky, confrontational cadence that is fast becoming—as attested to by the rowdies at KFC—a common speech style among young black males. Similarly, the arm-slinging, hand-hurling gestures of rap performers have made their way into many young blacks' casual gesticulations, becoming integral to their self-expression. The problem with such speech and mannerisms is that they make potential employers wary of young black men and can impede a young black's ability to interact comfortably with co-workers and customers. The black community has gone through too much to sacrifice upward mobility to the passing kick of an adversarial hip-hop "identity."

For those who insist that even the invisible structures of society reinforce racism, the burden of proof should rest with them to explain why hip-hop's bloody and sexist lyrics and videos and the criminal behavior of many rappers wouldn't have a negative effect upon whites' conception of black people.

At 2 A.M. on the New York subway not long ago, I saw another scene that captures the essence of rap's destructiveness. A young black man entered the car and began to rap loudly—profanely, arrogantly—with the usual wild gestures. This went on for five irritating minutes. When no one paid attention, he moved on to another car, all the while spouting his doggerel. This was what this young black man presented as his message to the world—his oratory, if you will.

Anyone who sees such behavior as a path to a better future—anyone, like Professor Dyson, who insists that hip-hop is an urgent "critique of a society that produces the need for the thug persona"—should step back and ask himself just where, exactly, the civil rights–era blacks might have gone wrong in lacking a hip-hop revolution. They created the world of equality, striving and success I live and thrive in.

Hip-hop creates nothing.

Periodical Bibliography

The following articles have been selected to supplement the diverse views presented in this chapter.

Steve Burgess — "Forced to Watch: Reality TV," January 26, 2004. www.thetyee.ca.

Susan J. Douglas — "We Are What We Watch," *In These Times*, July 1, 2004.

Kevin Downey — "A Dreamer of Dreams: Burnett Launched a Television Genre and Has Seen It Gain Respect," *Broadcasting & Cable*, January 19, 2004.

Irene Rosenberg Javors — "Hip-Hop Culture: Images of Gender and Gender Roles," *Annals of the American Psychotherapy Association*, Summer 2004.

Joan Morgan — "Sex, Lies, and Videos: The Images We See in Today's Hip-Hop Videos Are Making Our Girls Feel Less than the Sum of Their Parts," *Essence*, June 2002.

Jay Nordlinger — "Bang: Guns, Rap, and Silence—Violence in Rap Music," *National Review*, April 16, 2001.

Bill O'Reilly — "Poverty-Inducing Entertainment," January 18, 2003. www.townhall.com.

James Pinkerton — "Eminem: Violence as an Art Form," *Cincinnati Post*, November 8, 2002.

Joy Press — "My Big Fat Obnoxious Prank: The Lawless and Ever-Expanding World of Hidden-Camera TV," *Village Voice*, February 18–24, 2004.

Francine Prose — "Voting Democracy Off the Island: Reality TV and the Republican Ethos," *Harper's Magazine*, March 2004.

Erik Rush — "Rap Is Crap," May 16, 2003. www.worldnet.daily.com.

Crispin Sartwell — "Violence and Culture: Breaking the Rules OK in Video Games," *Atlanta Journal-Constitution*, January 9, 2002.

Patrick J. Shanahan — "'Married by America' and Other Signs of Cultural Decay," March 16, 2003. www.commonconservative.com.

Cynthia G. Wagner — "Aggression and Violent Media: Playing Video Games May Lead to More Violence than Watching TV," *Futurist*, July/August 2004.

CHAPTER 2

Is Popular Culture Too Coarse?

Chapter Preface

Complaints about the coarseness of popular culture are not new. Throughout history people have become shocked and outraged when new forms of popular entertainment emerge. Indeed, today's laments about the decline of culture have echoes in the distant past.

In ancient Greece, many songs performed in plays were deemed obscene by some. The plays of Aristophanes, now considered part of the foundation of modern drama, were offensive to some because of their depiction of controversial subjects. For example, in the comedy *Lysistrata*, the women of Athens and Sparta deny their husbands sexual contact to force them to end a war.

In 1594 the Lord Mayor of London requested (and was denied) permission from Queen Elizabeth to destroy all theaters because they were meeting places for undesirables. Other critics went so far as to blame the plays themselves for teaching and inspiring immoral behavior merely by depicting it. In 1583 Phillip Stubbes, a Puritan critic of theater, wrote a tract entitled "The Anatomic of Abuses" in which he argued that "if you will learn to play the hypocrite, to cog, lie and falsify . . . you need no other school, for all these good examples you may see painted before your eyes in plays."

The advent of motion pictures produced many outraged critics who feared cinema's impact on the masses. In 1901 a member of the British Parliament complained of the content of a mutoscope, a primitive type of film composed of a sequence of photographs arranged around the perimeter of a drum. The turn of a handle flipped the cards rapidly, giving the impression of movement. He lamented that one mutoscope, *Why Marie Put Out the Light*, featured "nude female figures [and] . . . as the pictures are all moving, it makes them more dangerous in their influence." In Germany in 1910 a pastor named Walter Conradt also attacked the emerging art form for its degrading impact. He examined 250 films and reported fifty-one adulteries, nineteen seductions, and ninety-seven murders. He concluded that censorship was necessary.

When rock-and-roll music exploded on the American scene in the 1950s in the form of Elvis Presley, his performances were widely criticized as vulgar and corrupting. He was famously filmed from the waist up on the Ed Sullivan TV show to prevent impressionable youths from seeing him gyrate his hips as he sang. After a 1957 concert in Los Angeles, critic Dick Williams wrote in the *Los Angeles Mirror-News* that the show was a "corruption of the innocent" and "a lesson in pornography," comparable to "one of those screeching uninhibited party rallies which Nazis used to hold for Hitler." Elsewhere, protests were staged during which Presley records were smashed or burned. By today's standards, his performances would be considered tame.

The same battles over the decline of popular culture from years ago continue to rage today. In the following viewpoints some authors attack popular culture for its coarseness and vulgarity while others dismiss those complaints as overreactions.

> "*Enough is enough. As a parent and an FCC Commissioner, I share the public's disgust with increasingly crude radio and television content.*"

Television Programming Has Become Increasingly Coarse

Jonathan S. Adelstein

In the following viewpoint Jonathan S. Adelstein contends that the tasteless advertising and halftime entertainment during the 2004 Super Bowl are clear examples of the coarsening of television programming. He argues that broadcasters must be held responsible for vulgar content, and local broadcasters should be able to reject programming that is offensive to their communities. Jonathan S. Adelstein is a commissioner on the Federal Communications Commission.

As you read, consider the following questions:
1. According to Adelstein, what was offensive about some of the advertising during the 2004 Super Bowl?
2. What is the FCC's legitimate role in restricting indecent conduct, according to the author?
3. According to the author, how is the FCC limited in its ability to regulate content, and what other organizations must share responsibility?

Jonathan S. Adelstein, testimony before the U.S. Senate Committee on Commerce, Science, and Transportation, Washington, DC, February 11, 2004.

L ike many of you, I sat down with my wife and children to watch the [2004] Super Bowl. I was expecting a showcase of America's best talent, both on and off the field, and the apotheosis of our cultural creativity during the entertainment and advertising portions. Instead, like millions of others, I was appalled by the halftime show, not just for the shock-value stunt at the end,[1] but for the overall raunchy performance displayed in front of so many children; one in five American children were watching, according to reports. And the advertising set a new low for what should air during family time.

The Super Bowl is a rare occasion for families to get together to enjoy a national pastime everyone should be able to appreciate. Instead, a special family occasion was truly disrespected.

Tasteless Commercials

I could highlight any number of tasteless commercials that depicted sexual and bodily functions in a vile manner. Any sense of internal controls appeared out the window, so long as the advertiser paid the multi-million dollar rate.

One commercial that really stung my family, and many other parents with whom I spoke, was a violent trailer for an unrated horror movie. It showed horrible monsters with huge fangs attacking people. I literally jumped out of my chair to get between the TV and my three-year-old. Other parents told me they couldn't reach for the remote control fast enough. I wonder how those who chose to broadcast such violence can sleep at night when they gave so many American children nightmares.

No parent should have to jump in front of the TV to block their children from such images, whether during a commercial or a halftime show. No parent should feel guilty for not being with their child every single moment in case they need to block the TV during what most would consider to be a family viewing event.

The entire Super Bowl broadcast was punctuated by inappropriate images that were an embarrassment for our coun-

1. Singer Janet Jackson had her breast bared by another performer.

try. The halftime show, with its global appeal, was a wasted opportunity to showcase the best that U.S. culture has to offer. The U.S. has the world's greatest musical culture to promote across the globe, and that includes the many artists who performed at the event. Our musicians and artists offer a vibrant musical melting pot that expands our horizons and enriches our culture. As a musician myself, I am proud of artists who everyday express their creativity without trying to one up each other in shock value. There is plenty of magnificent talent here for the whole family to enjoy. It is those performances that broadcasters should showcase. Instead, the halftime show needlessly descended into lewdness and crassness.

This latest incident is only the tip of the iceberg. There is nearly universal concern about the state of our public airwaves. I personally received more than 10,000 emails last week [February 2004], and the FCC [Federal Communications Commission] received more than 200,000. But that pales in comparison to the number of people who over the past year expressed their outrage to me about the homogenization and crassness of the media. The public is outraged by the increasingly crude content they see and hear in their media today. They are fed up with the sex, violence, and profanity flooding into our homes. Just this month at an FCC hearing in San Antonio, a member of the audience expressed concern with indecency on Spanish-language television novellas.

Complaints are exploding that our airwaves are increasingly dominated by graphic and shocking entertainment. Some observe that broadcasters are only responding to competition from cable programming. Take MTV, a cable network known for pushing the envelope. It's owned by Viacom, which also owns CBS. It's no coincidence that MTV produced the halftime show. But the network thoughtlessly applied the cable programmer's standards during the Super Bowl, the ultimate family event.

As a musician, I recognize that channels like MTV have a place in our society. I also understand and respect that many would prefer that they not intrude into the mainstream of American family life. Parents who purchase cable television have the legal right to block any channel they don't consider appropriate for their children. More parents should be made aware of this right. Free over-the-air broadcasting, however, offers no such alternative to parents. For broadcast material designed for mature audiences, it's a matter of the right time and place.

Enough Is Enough

Enough is enough. As a parent and an FCC Commissioner, I share the public's disgust with increasingly crude radio and television content.

Carlson. © 1996 *Milwaukee Journal Sentinel*. Reproduced by permission of Universal Press Syndicate.

I've only served on the Commission for about a year, but I'm proud that we've stepped up our enforcement in that time. And we need to ramp it up even further. In my view, gratuitous use of swear words or nudity have no place in broadcasting. We need to act forcefully now. Not surprisingly, complaints before the FCC are rising rapidly, with more than 240,000 complaints covering 370 programs last year. In the cases on which I have voted, I have supported going to the statutory maximum for fines. But even this statutory maximum—$27,500 per incident—is woefully inadequate. I welcome the efforts by Congress to authorize us to increase fines substantially across all our areas of jurisdiction.

Awaiting such authority, I've pushed for new approaches to deter indecency. We can increase the total amount of fines by fining for each separate utterance within the same program segment. And we need to hold hearings to consider revoking broadcasters' licenses in serious, repeated cases. I worked last April to have the FCC put broadcasters on notice that we were taking these steps to establish a stronger enforcement regime. Our challenge now is to act more quickly when we get complaints, and to ensure that our complaint procedures are as consumer-friendly as possible.

The FCC's Limits

But there are limits to what the FCC can do. We must balance strict enforcement of the indecency laws with the First Amendment. If we overstep, we risk losing the narrow constitutional authority we now have to enforce the rules. Nevertheless, many cases I have seen in my tenure are so far past any boundary of decency that any broadcaster should have known the material would violate our rules.

So it may very well take more than the FCC to turn this around. We are not the only ones with a public trust to keep the airwaves free from obscene, indecent and profane material. Broadcasters are given exclusive rights to use the public airwaves in the public interest. The broadcasters themselves bear much of the responsibility to keep our airwaves decent. As stewards of the airwaves, broadcasters are in the position to step up and use their public airwaves in a manner that celebrates our country's tremendous cultural heritage. Or they can continue down the path of debasing that heritage. Their choices ultimately will guide our enforcement.

Serving local communities is the cornerstone of the broadcaster's social compact with the public. When people choose to become licensed broadcasters, they understand that a public service responsibility comes with that privilege. In his famous remarks lamenting the "vast wasteland" of television, Newton Minow rightly observed that, "an investment in broadcasting is buying a share in public responsibility." Every broadcaster should take that to heart. Public responsibility may mean passing up an opportunity to pander to the nation's whims and current ratings trends when it is more important to stand up and meet the needs of the local community.

Corporate Responsibility

Broadcasters need to show more corporate responsibility. They must rise above commercial pressures, and recognize the broader social problems they may be compounding.

Many factors set the cultural and moral tone of our society. I welcome the attention that our indecency enforcement is receiving. I don't think of it as silly or overblown, as some have suggested. The question before America is whether the coarsening of our media is responsible for the coarsening of our culture, or vice versa. My answer is both. They feed on each other.

Media consolidation only intensifies the pressures. Fast-growing conglomerates focus on the bottom line above all else. The FCC should reconsider its dramatic weakening of media ownership limits [in 2003].

Local broadcasters also need the ability to reject network programming that doesn't meet their communities' standards. The FCC must preserve the critical back-and-forth local affiliates have with the networks in the fight against indecency.

In terms of taking positive steps, the FCC can do more to help families. Because our particular focus today is on children, one vital step is completing a pending rulemaking on children's television obligations of digital television. The FCC started this proceeding more than three years ago, yet it remains unfinished. We should quickly complete this proceeding to help meet children's educational needs, and give parents tools to help their children make appropriate viewing choices.

During the Super Bowl, and on far too many other occasions, people feel assaulted by what is broadcast at them. My job is to protect our families from the broadcast of obscene, indecent or profane material. That also means promoting healthy fare for our children. After all, the airwaves are owned by the American people, and the public is eager to take some control back.

"The moral guardians of the nation's airwaves, predators one and all, for the time being have the upper hand—and know it."

Cultural Conservatives Exaggerate the Coarseness of Television Programming

Carl F. Horowitz

In the following viewpoint Carl F. Horowitz argues that cultural conservatives overreact to controversial moments on television such as the halftime show of the 2004 Super Bowl, during which singer Janet Jackson had her breast bared by another performer. According to Horowitz, the far right is engaged in a culture war to impose their religious values on the country, and many legislators are listening to them. Horowitz contends that conservatives use incidents such as the Jackson debacle to generate controversy, which fuels their writing and television careers. Carl F. Horowitz is a consultant on labor, immigration, welfare reform, and housing issues.

As you read, consider the following questions:
1. According to Horowitz, how was the CBS decision not to air a film about the Reagans related to the crusade against indecency on television?
2. Why are cultural conservatives predators, according to Horowitz?
3. According to the author, how has Congress responded to the complaints of cultural conservatives?

Carl F. Horowitz, "Post–Super Bowl Cultural Conservatism: Personal Foul, Piling On," www.lewrockwell.com, March 6, 2004. Copyright © 2004 by Carl F. Horowitz. Reproduced by permission of the publisher and author.

Cultural conservatives in this country seem afflicted with a bad case of short-term memory loss. Only a few months ago [November 2003], if you recall, they were nearly leaping over each other to congratulate CBS television for its eleventh-hour decision to yank the scheduled mini-series, "The Reagans," and move the presentation to the much-less-watched Showtime cable channel. Never mind that the made-for-TV film's "attack" on President [Ronald] Reagan's legacy consisted of maybe a combined half-minute's worth of dialogue, and in any event was tame stuff compared to what almost everyone on the Left (and a good many on the Right) today say about President George W. Bush. Never mind either that most of the people who denounced the movie never bothered to see it in the first place. CBS did the right thing, and thus deserved a round of applause.

Some people might not see much of a connection between coaxing CBS into pulling the plug of that mini-series and grilling that network this February [2004] (and no doubt for many months to come) in the wake of its failure to vet in advance the [2004] Super Bowl halftime choreography gaffe. That's a pity, really. Look beneath the surface, and think. A predator, knowing prey has succumbed once before, typically will attack a second time—and a third, fourth and fifth time, until finally (one hopes) the prey engages in healthy self-defense. Human beings, to say nothing of the lower species, have operated on this principle for millennia.

Morality Police

The moral guardians of the nation's airwaves, predators one and all, for the time being have the upper hand—and know it. There's seemingly no end to the bowing and scraping they seek from TV executives for "allowing" Justin Timberlake to rip away Janet Jackson's blouse at the end of the song, "Rock Your Body." They view the exposure, whether planned or spontaneous, of a pasty on one of Ms. Jackson's breasts for the duration of perhaps three nanoseconds as posing a mortal threat to America's families. CBS, they warn, had better clean up its act or heads will roll. CBS's sister network, MTV, which produced the halftime show, ought to heed the same message, as should the two networks' parent company, Viacom. In fact, so should the NFL and the offending performing artists. As for other entertainment industry bigwigs, the message is clear: *Don't mess with us.*

Major media, ever edgy about a pending FCC [Federal Communications Commission] crackdown, predictably have chosen damage control over principle. Here's the body count over the last several weeks [February and March 2004]:

- MTV bumped seven of its videos from prime time.
- CBS instituted a five-minute tape delay for its broadcast of the Grammy awards show; Viacom is now outfitting all of its radio and TV stations with the same capability.
- Janet Jackson was cut from the televised Grammy Awards presentation.
- Clear Channel Communications, Inc., which owns more than 1,200 radio stations, fired a radio talk-show host for a sexually explicit skit, "Bubba the Love Sponge." The skit, which had aired on four Florida outlets, had prompted the FCC to recommend $755,000 in fines, which the network just recently agreed to pay.
- Clear Channel, with its new "zero-tolerance" policy, announced it no longer would run Howard Stern's syndicated radio program on the half-dozen of its stations carrying it (Stern's parent company, Infinity Broadcasting, like CBS and MTV, is part of Viacom).
- California's Laguna Beach High School pulled out of an agreement to let MTV film a reality show based on its students' lives.

Do the words "chilling effect" come into mind?

Right-Wing Culture Warriors

The nuttier fringes of the Right also have gone on the warpath. A Tennessee woman filed suit [the suit was later dropped] in federal court in Knoxville against Janet Jackson, Justin Timberlake, CBS, MTV and Viacom, seeking damages from each party. Excuse me, but exactly who was harmed by the halftime show? Was it the cheering fans inside Houston's Reliant Stadium, oblivious to the "pornography" in front of them? Or maybe it was the 90 million or so American TV viewers? Punitive damages, the suit read, should be set no higher than what the parties made out of participating in the Super Bowl. And get this—any additional punitive damages should not exceed the gross annual revenues of each defendant for the last three years. In other words, we're talking about extracting *no more than* tens of billions, possibly hundreds of billions, of dollars from the defendants.

Let the Free Market Function

Today, the first response to any controversy is, 'there ought to be a law.' But in matters of morality and freedom of speech, it is best for law to be the very last recourse society considers. The first resort is to let freedom and the free market function.

Wendy McElroy, www.foxnews.com, February 18, 2004.

The culture-war types long have specialized in making molehills into mountains, all the better to boost their flaky profiles. What's different this time is that they have a true-blue friend in the Federal Communications Commission. FCC Chairman Michael Powell, in testimony February 11 before the House Energy and Commerce Subcommittee on Telecommunications and the Internet, called the show "a new low for prime-time television . . . the latest example in a growing list of deplorable incidents over the nation's airwaves." As the son of Secretary of State Colin Powell, you can be sure he sees this as his time to shine, to dispel any doubts he's a tough, no-nonsense guy like his father. He's already announced his intention to reverse an FCC decision that had let U2 singer Bono off the hook for using the word "f——ing" (as an adjective) back in January 2003 at the Golden Globe Awards. The other four commissioners—Kathleen Abernathy, Michael Copps, Kevin Martin, and Jonathan Adelstein—each have demonstrated a propensity for not making waves.

Lawmakers Caving In

Lawmakers are doing much more than hearing testimony. Subcommittee Chairman Rep. Fred Upton, R-Mich., a week and a half prior to the Super Bowl already had introduced legislation, the Broadcast Decency Enforcement Act of 2004 (H.R. 3717) [the legislation is pending], to increase tenfold the maximum FCC per-incident fine for indecency violations from $27,500 to $275,000. The Super Bowl brouhaha provided just the lift to put the bill on the fast track. At the hearing Upton minced no words about the need for federal muscle:

This is a tough bill which, if enacted, would help clean up our airwaves, no doubt about it. It's just that, regrettably, the current "race to the bottom" in the entertainment industry has made it an all but impossible task for parents. They should be able to rely on the fact that—at times when their children are likely to be tuning in—broadcast television and radio programming will be free of indecency, obscenity and profanity.

Nor was this smug, pompous tyrant through. He warned of dire consequences for those not falling into line:

We need to look at the level of the fines. We need to look at beefing up the license renewal procedures to ensure that indecency violations are factored in by the FCC. As I've suggested before, perhaps we are at the point where we need to drop the hammer of three strikes and you're off the air.

Rep. Heather Wilson, R-N.M., taunted Viacom President Mel Karmazin at the hearing. "You knew what you were doing," she said. "You wanted us all to be abuzz. It improves your ratings. It improves your market share and it lines your pockets." (Surely Wilson, who holds a Ph.D. from Oxford, could have shown a bit more sophistication!) Karmazin's response was to whip out a white flag: "I take responsibility that it aired. Shame on me." Apparently, contrition didn't pay off. On March 3 the full Energy and Commerce Committee approved the Upton measure by 47-1, but with one major difference: The maximum FCC fine was now up to $500,000.

Meanwhile, House Majority Leader Tom DeLay, R-Tex, got downright threatening in a televised March 2 speech before the National Association of Broadcasters:

The television industry, like every other industry, works best when it regulates and polices itself. But if the entertainment industry cannot pull itself together and stay within some boundaries of decency, Congress will have no choice but to step in. Make no mistake: If decision makers at studios, networks and affiliates fail to appreciate the sensitivity of the post–Super Bowl environment, the consequences will not be merely economic.

Apparently DeLay is blind to the irony that it is people such as he who single-handedly created this "environment.". . .
Genuine friends of liberty logically recoil at the prospect

of a federal investigation to Get To The Bottom Of This. While such a reaction is welcome, I find it insufficient. For even *without* government intervention, the hysterically orchestrated reaction to the halftime show may well result in a highly censorious artistic climate. In order to understand why, it is necessary first to understand a few things about the *modus operandi* of the traditionalist mind, especially as it resides in and around Washington, D.C., and why it so often incites rather than enlightens audiences.

Culture-war pundits are, by natural inclination, pugilists. They thrive on conflict; indeed, they cannot bear to live without it. Whenever there is an "incident" in literature, the arts or some other arena of culture to exploit for political gain, however trivial, they wildly inflate its importance. Part of the explanation for this is career ambition. These are people who make a living in newspaper, television, radio, think tank, lobbying and government circles—and very often more than one at the same time. To generate controversy is to generate readers, viewers, contributors, and maybe even a book contract. But arguably a greater reason for the combativeness is the prospect of combat itself. Exaggerating the menace posed by a Robert Mapplethorpe [homoerotic] photograph or a Britney Spears song, for example, gives them a sense of importance, of being first among equals in the world of ideas. To observe [conservative columnist] Ann Coulter on the warpath (and when is she not?) is to observe someone whose existence revolves around picking fights.

Related to this propensity, these pundits share a near-consensus opinion that America's cultural sky is falling. Encapsulated, the story goes something like this. For 40 years, ever since roughly the Beatles' first appearance on the "Ed Sullivan Show," there has been a ruthless assault by mass media (also known as "the culture") against family, community, religion and schools. Consequently, our now-hedonistic country has been rotting from within. Whereas in an earlier era we could quarantine and clean up cultural "pollution" emanating from New York, Hollywood and various college campuses, in the current era we poor Americans, our moral antibodies all but depleted, have virtually ceded control of our country to immoral elites. The grievances of Americans as yet seduced by counterculture pied pipers thus must be articulated before we all wind up in a sewer. End of story.

Now even at its best, this view is highly spurious. But as hammy, splenetic, media-hungry personalities like Coulter, not to mention [conservatives] Cal Thomas, Rush Limbaugh, Michael Savage, and Sean Hannity, advance it, this critique typically has all the intellectual rigor of a bad high-school essay.

Holding a view is one thing; convincing large audiences of that view's soundness is another. Toward that end conservative opinion-shapers have developed a propagandistic method for winning converts. They first pick and choose, as if by committee, an Incident—a moral smoking gun with which to indict all of contemporary America. Then they write editorials or give speeches. . . . Their canned response to the Super Bowl incident is a textbook example. . . .

Opposition to censorship, whether of the official or informal kind, must be the overriding principle for any supporter of liberty. That means, inevitably, doing battle with the censors. There's no way out of this. Libertarians should forget about their purity, get in the trenches, and fight. Write the FCC. The commission listens to citizens who favor censorship; they also will listen to those who oppose it. E-mail your Congressman and tell him to vote against H.R. 3717 (and soon—the full-floor vote may come up any day). Flood the White House switchboard with calls, since President [George W.] Bush has expressed his support. Get involved and protest. If you allow the moral bullies to seize the high ground, they will.

I might mention in passing something about the Super Bowl perhaps lost amid all the controversy: The New England Patriots defeated the Carolina Panthers, 32-29, in a down-to-the-wire thriller. But, hey, who cares about a mere game of football when "the culture" needs cleaning up?

"Listeners seem to expect outrageous behavior from radio announcers. Radio managers seem to think their stations benefit from publicity, even if it's negative publicity."

Radio Broadcasting Has Become Increasingly Vulgar

Frank Absher

Frank Absher argues in the following viewpoint that radio shock jocks are broadcasting increasingly obscene material. He states that today's broadcasters lack the talent of their predecessors and rely on shocking the audience for ratings. He also argues that in addition to broadcasters and radio station general managers, radio audiences are to blame for this for not insisting on better quality and standards. Frank Absher is a former radio broadcast personality and founder of the St. Louis Media Archives.

As you read, consider the following questions:

1. According to Absher, what sorts of material are accepted as entertainment in radio today?
2. Why was the quality of radio broadcasting higher in the past, according to Absher?
3. According to the author, can the state of radio be improved?

Frank Absher, "Will Radio Ever Grow Up?" *St. Louis Journalism Review*, vol. 33, January 2003, p. 22. Copyright © 2003 by *St. Louis Journalism Review*. Reproduced by permission.

Two New York disc jockeys thought it would be clever to broadcast the sounds of a couple having intercourse inside St. Patrick's Cathedral. Even though no Federal Communications Commission (FCC) regulations were broken, the public outcry forced the radio station to fire the disc jockeys.

A morning announcer in Phoenix broadcast a phone conversation he had with Darryl Kile's[1] widow in which he told her she was hot and asked if she had a date for the ball game. He broke the FCC rule against airing a phone conversation without first getting the permission of the other party. He was fired by management—not for breaking the rule but because major advertisers started canceling their business with the station. To date, no complaints have been filed with the FCC over the improper broadcast of the phone conversation, so it appears the station won't be penalized.

Two Nashville disc jockeys were suspended after they sent an intern out in a car, telling him to crash it into a wall to see how fast he had to go before the air bag deployed. They had taken the bag out of the car.

A syndicated host out of Chicago made references to "oral sex, genitalia, masturbation, ejaculation and excretory activities" and saw his parent company fined $21,000 for his conduct. He said, "Life on the edge ain't always easy. If you don't take chances, you don't make advances."

Welcome to what passes for creativity and entertainment in radio today.

Vulgarity Is Common

If there is anything "wrong" with the incidents described above, it's that they are becoming more commonplace. Listeners seem to expect outrageous behavior from radio announcers. Radio managers seem to think their stations benefit from publicity, even if it's negative publicity. But, what about ethics or conscience?

Scott Shannon, a nationally known program director and radio veteran, recently told the Associated Press, "For the stations and the shows that do these kinds of stunts, there certainly has been a re-examination of conscience, attitudes

---

1. Kile was a major league baseball player who died in 2002 at the age of 33.

and guidelines." There is, however, little overt evidence of a sea of change in radio.

No less a figure than Ron Jacobs, known as the granddaddy of KHJ's (Los Angeles) success in establishing the Drake Format as the rock format of the late '60s/early '70s, draws an interesting analogy between today's "talent" and the deejays he oversaw: "It's like comparing the creativity of a kid on the street flashing a bus with the creativity of Johnny Carson." Jacobs remembers when you could turn on the radio and hear "mature guys doing classy things."

Shock Jocks Coarsen Our Culture

Commercial rewards drive the creation, production, and marketing of ever more Howard Sterns, Greasemans, and the rest of the shock jocks. This inevitably leads to a coarsening of our culture, which has particularly harmful effects on children.

Ralph Nader, *The Nader Page*, July 14, 1999.

But, maybe listeners don't want intelligent, mature, classy radio announcers today. In the wake of the above-mentioned stunts, Edison Research and Jacobs Media conducted a poll of listeners, the results of which were published in the Nov. 1 [2002] issue of *Radio & Records*. The survey questions were posted on the websites of more than 20 of the country's rock stations, and there were more than 7,300 responses.

Only 28 percent of the respondents agreed with the phrase "Shock jock radio personalities have gone too far." In fact, respondents were twice as likely to tune in to shows where the announcer pushed the limits of good taste. Several announcers stated that anyone who was offended should simply listen to another station.

Given these numbers, it stands to reason that radio management would seek out announcers who say or do controversial things. Kevin Metheny programs the Clear Channel cluster in Cleveland. He told *R&R*, "We anticipate that certain high-profile talent will draw a lot of fire. We want to be a magnet for the most remarkable, compelling, difficult-to-duplicate radio talent in the world." He also told the magazine, "The point is not to frivolously insult people or offend their sensibilities; the point is to entertain."

The Role of Station Owners

Some feel the station owners should shoulder a big part of the blame for what radio has become. Dave Sniff, program director of KFMB in San Diego, is quoted in another *R&R* article: "Infinity and Westwood One are no strangers to this style of radio. . . . They not only know that controversy will follow, they expect it and, most likely, will celebrate it when it happens."

For more than 45 years, Curt Brown has worn just about every hat in the business in Springfield, Mo. For 31 of those years he was general manager of KTTS-AM and FM. His take on the whole situation of what passes for "entertainment" on the radio today is one of confusion—just as it is for many of us: "The trend of using people who tell T&A jokes while some buffoon laughs in the background has caused many people to be less than thrilled with radio today. Why has radio assumed a leadership role in smut media offerings? Is it because there was no place else to go?"

So, there's enough blame for the current state of radio to be spread around to everyone. The radio we have today is, to paraphrase Jimmy Buffett, "our own damn fault." If we weren't listening to it, station management would have to give us something else, and just about anything would be an improvement. But don't get your hopes up.

Ethics? Conscience? Ron Jacobs summed it up: "Radio was happening in the 20th century. It stopped being innovative in the 1990s. There is no hope of it being rescued."

"Today the government censor's target is language judged to be obscene. Tomorrow? Who knows?"

Efforts to Censor Radio Vulgarity Are Misguided

Neal Boortz

According to Neal Boortz in the following viewpoint, the radio broadcasts of shock jocks such as Howard Stern do no real harm to anyone. Boortz argues that the Federal Communications Commission's crackdown on obscene language in radio broadcasts is inappropriate, and could lead to real threats to the First Amendment. Asking the government to censor to avoid being offended is misguided, he contends. Neal Boortz is a lawyer and nationally syndicated radio talk show host.

As you read, consider the following questions:

1. According to the author, how should people respond to radio programming they consider to be offensive?
2. What are the implications of restrictions on political advertising, according to Boortz?
3. What Supreme Court case does the author mention to illustrate the current climate of censorship?

Neal Boortz, "The Federal Censorship Commission," www.townhall.com, April 23, 2004. Copyright © 2004 by Neal Boortz. Reproduced by permission.

[R]adio shock jock] Howard Stern has been doing what he has been doing, vulgar as it can be, for 20 years. I've searched to the ends of the Internet and as many of Nebraska's best weekly's as I could, and I have yet to turn up one story about one single human being anywhere in this vast country of ours who was in any way harmed by anything they heard from a radio dialed to Stern. Not once have I heard even whispers of a situation where a Howard Stern broadcast violated any individual's right to life, liberty or property.

The FCC on the Rampage

The FCC (Federal Censorship Commission)[1] is on a roll, radio station owners are in a state of near panic, and broadcasters are losing their livelihoods. Some FCC commissioners, most notably Michael Copp, (a Democrat, by the way), have decided that the FCC has a much broader roll to fill in monitoring and managing the content of radio and television broadcasts than previously imagined.

Americans suffering from AHD (Acute Hypersensitivity Disorder)[2] are fueling the situation, eagerly writing letters and voicing complaints whenever they hear something come from their radio that offends them. A new right is being claimed, the right to not be offended. Politicians anxious to retain their positions of privilege and power in an election year goad the FCC on.

Pat Boone, a musical icon of the '70's, has chimed in. Still smarting over the failure of the keepers of the community standards to derail the rise of that fanny-wiggling upstart from Tupelo,[3] Boone shares with us his belief that government is just grand.

It is not the role of the government to determine what we can or cannot listen to on the radio. For adults, it's a matter of choice. For children, it's a matter left up to parents. Every modern radio I have ever seen has a minimum of two knobs. Votes for or against programming can be cast with a simple twist of either one. And please spare me your concerns that our precious children might inadvertently hear something

1. The FCC's proper name is the Federal Communications Commission. 2. AHD actually stands for Acute Hyperactivity Disorder. 3. Elvis Presley

ugly while out of your control. Believe me, nothing they hear on the radio is going to match today's lunch line and playground whispers and snickers at the local government school. Besides, just how many simulated murders did your child watch on television the last week? Isn't it time for you to schedule a parenting priority check?

The FCC Violates Our Right to Free Speech

In this headlong rush to expand the government's authority over the media, no one has paused to consider whether the government should have such authority in the first place. No one has noticed that the very existence of the FCC is a flagrant violation of the right to free speech.

Robert Garmong, *Capitalism Magazine*, September 26, 2004.

Today the government censor's target is language judged to be obscene. Tomorrow? Who knows? We already have heard that some think the FCC censorship crusade should be expanded to satellite and cable. Somehow Tony Soprano saying "darn you" doesn't seem all that realistic. What's next? Comedy clubs?

What Is Offensive?

To some, foul language is offensive. For me there are political ideas that I find far more offensive than any dirty joke I've ever heard. The phrase "President Hillary Clinton" immediately comes to mind. That very idea disturbs me far more than any scatological or sexual reference I could imagine coming from the dashboard of my car. In fact, I had to write this particular paragraph in the early morning to give my mind time to purge the idea of a President Hillary before turning it into nightmares at the end of the day.

So . . . if I find talk of the political heroes of the left to be offensive, even dangerous, why should I be subject to that drivel on the radio? Where is my government protection? Do you think I'm overreaching here? I don't think so. In the current climate of censorship it is not such a stretch to imagine the government exercising censorship of political thought in broadcasting. In fact, it's already here. Remember, please, that the U.S. Supreme Court, in one of its most dangerous and vile decisions ever, has decided that the provisions of the Campaign Finance Reform act prohibiting certain political advertising on radio or television in close proximity to elections is quite Constitutional, thank you very much (for nothing). So, for those of you who don't believe that the role of FCC censorship could expand to expressions of political thought, why don't you take a shot at explaining to me why, if it is legal for the congress to pass a law restricting political advertising, politicians couldn't pass a law restricting the expression of certain political ideas immediately prior to an election altogether.

A Threat to the First Amendment

This threat extends even beyond sexual and political thought. If it is appropriate for the government to protect us from the expression of offensive sexual matter, why not extend that protection to thoughts on any social issues that offend? My expressions of disagreement with affirmative action offend those who benefit from this system of government mandated racial discrimination. Should I be forbidden from expressing those views? Some would certainly support that idea. And nowhere is the negative listener reaction stronger than when I accuse the millions of parents who have replaced effective parenting and discipline with Ritalin of child abuse. Maybe that topic should be forbidden also.

Americans have bought into the ridiculous concept of "public ownership of the airwaves," an idea created by politicians for no purpose other than to legitimize government control. We are now at the point where the vast majority of people in the United States get their daily dose of news and information on just what the government and politicians are up to from agencies that are licensed by that very government! We are now seeing that control over those licenses can and will be used to control content. Today the concentration is on content of a sexual nature, but the seeds for control of political content have already germinated. Do you feel any funny vibrations coming from the graves of our founding fathers?

"Now pimp glorification has come to center stage in rapperland."

Rap Music's Focus on Pimps Harms Society

Clarence Page

In the following viewpoint Clarence Page argues that hip-hop artists are glorifying pimps and the casual sex implied by those references to prostitution. Although some rappers claim that their use of the word *pimp* is benign, Page points out that rappers frequently use misogynistic lyrics that imply that women are prostitutes. The pimp culture promoted by rap music, Page argues, is partially responsible for the rise in out-of-wedlock births in the black community. Clarence Page is a syndicated columnist and member of the editorial staff of the *Chicago Tribune*.

As you read, consider the following questions:

1. According to Page, what does the sale of a beverage called Pimp Juice say about pop culture?
2. How has Queen Latifah countered mysogynistic lyrics, according to the author?
3. In Page's view, what heroes should young people look up to?

Clarence Page, "Hearing Hip-Hop's Pathetic Message," *Jewish World Review*, September 16, 2003. Copyright © 2003 by *Jewish World Review*. Reproduced by permission.

As marketing schemes go, the hip-hop star Nelly risks sending a lot of mixed signals with the name of the new energy drink he is marketing.

Pimp Juice

It's called "Pimp Juice."

I could be wrong, but Pimp Juice does not sound to me like something that you want to put in your mouth.

Either way, you won't get a chance to find out if the leaders of some black community organizations have their way.

In Los Angeles last week [September 2003], Project Islamic HOPE, the National Alliance for Positive Action and the National Black Anti-Defamation League staged a press conference to urge the removal of the rapper's energy drink from store shelves.

In Chicago, the Rev. Michael Pfleger, pastor of St. Sabina Catholic Church, threatened to boycott any store that carried the drink.

In Durham, N.C., the Rev. Paul Scott, founder of Messianic Afrikan Nation, said, "As black men we should be building a nation of strong black leaders, not a nation of superenergized, drunk pimps."

The complaint: Pimp Juice glorifies the world's second oldest profession, which is the employment of women working in the world's first oldest profession.

Nelly and his spokesmen beg to differ. In launching the drink on Sept. 1, Nelly said it was named after his hit song "Pimp Juice" from his 2002 multiplatinum album, "Nellyville." "Pimp juice is anything that attracts the opposite sex," Nelly said. "Whatever you [are] using to win with right now, that's your juice—that's your pimp juice, so keep pimping."

Well, maybe.

What the Word Really Means

Back in the prehistoric age before there was rap music or, for that matter, laptops or cell phones, my generation used such terms as "pimp walk," "pimp style" or simply "pimpin'" some sucker who didn't know any better. But we never had any confusion as to where the word came from.

Nor, it appears, do rappers, who too often refer to women

by the disrespectful term "ho," as in Ludacris' lyric "I've got ho's/In different area codes. . . ."

Queen Latifah, among other hip-hop icons, tried to nip such creeping misogyny (It means disrespect for women, children. Look it up.) in the bud. In her uplifting tune "U.N.I.T.Y.," she beseeches her sisters, "You gotta let him know . . . /You ain't a bitch or a ho."

Pimp Glorification

Now pimp glorification has come to center stage in rapper-land. The video for popular rapper 50 Cent's mega-hit "PIMP" portrays him as a novice pimp before the grand pimp council, presided over by rapper Snoop Dogg with his real-life se-quined "spiritual adviser," Bishop Don Magic Juan at his side.

Words That Can Scar

[Rappers] "50 Cent" and "Snoop Dogg" are leading children into a duplicitous lie, where pimps are some perverse anti-hero, as if the business of procuring women and girls as pros-titutes for profit is acceptable. Now in school, I must stop each student I hear discussing "bitch slappin" or "big pimpin" and give them a dose of reality of what those terms mean. Words are our means of communication, words carry impact and value and can scar and maim.

John F. Borowski, "Pimping the First Amendment," www.common dreams.org, October 16, 2004.

I remember the colorful bishop (who also appeared onstage with Snoop and "some faux ho's" at the recent MTV Video Music Awards show) from my days as a police reporter in Chicago back in the 1970s. He used to be the West Side's pimp supreme until he embraced another one of the world's oldest professions, preaching. Juan's playful "pimp style" is amusing these days, but he's hardly the sort of role model self-respecting parents want for their kids or their community.

Nelly's Pimp Juice seems like the last straw to those who are upset about out-of-wedlock birth rates in black communities, rates that leveled off in the late 1990s at close to 70 percent of live black births. Worse, soaring child abandonment rates have left millions of kids to grow up without the benefit of both parents.

And while out-of-wedlock births have leveled off among blacks, they have soared since the 1980s among whites to more than 25 percent, the rate that first caused alarm when it appeared among blacks in the mid-1960s.

Corporate Responsibility

It would be too easy, in my view, to blame the rise of irresponsible sex and the breakdown in parenthood on the media. But it also would be too easy to say that the industry doesn't have any impact at all. If the media can sell CDs and soft drinks, they can sell moral attitudes too.

There are many reasons why out-of-wedlock birth rates are rising. If pop culture is pumping out the message that pimpin' and irresponsible sex is cool, it is increasingly important that we bombard our young people with healthier messages too.

Just as my generation respected heroes like Martin Luther King, Malcolm X, Harriet Tubman, Medgar Evers and Mary McCloud Bethune, we should help today's youngsters find role models who can help them lift their eyes out of the gutter and aim them toward the stars.

The chief youth consultant in our house, also known as my 14-year-old son, once told me that "Kids can tell the difference between satire and seriousness, Dad."

In other words, kids don't necessarily follow rap stars as role models. True, but it also helps for them to know they have other choices.

> *"Whereas the old guard can only see literal pimps, many within the hip hop generation have redefined the word to suit the needs of the post–Civil Rights era world."*

Rap Music's Focus on Pimps Does Not Harm Society

Mark Anthony Neal

Mark Anthony Neal argues in the following viewpoint that rap artists have redefined the word *pimp* in a way that makes it less offensive. Neal claims that there is a long tradition of using aspects of the pimp image as a means of projecting masculinity. Contrary to critics' charges that rappers' focus on pimps degrades women and sex, hip-hop's embrace of the term attempts to empower African American men. Mark Anthony Neal is an associate professor of American studies at the University of Texas at Austin, and the author of *Songs in the Key of Black Life: A Rhythm and Blues Nation.*

As you read, consider the following questions:

1. According to Neal, how do some rappers defend their embrace of the pimp style?
2. What is the connection between pimps and clergy, according to Neal?
3. According to the author, how can the pimp culture in rap music be considered empowering?

Mark Anthony Neal, "Critical Noir: Pimpin' Ain't Easy," *Africana*, October 2, 2003. Copyright © 2003 by Africana.com, Inc. Reproduced by permission of the author.

Now, I'll be the first to admit that I cringed the first time I heard Nelly's song "Pimp Juice"—it was an automatic reaction to Nelly's attempt at a pimp-styled falsetto (see Paul Wingfield's "18 with a Bullet" for the definitive example) and the fact he would name *anything* pimp juice without even a hint of irony. A year later "Pimp Juice," also the name of Nelly's brand-new energy drink, is at the center of a controversy—one that again pits the Civil Rights old-guard (and their wannabe progeny) against the so-called hip hop generation. Nelly launched his new energy drink on September 1, 2003, telling folks "Pimp Juice is anything that attracts the opposite sex," adding that "whatever you're using to win with right now, that's your juice, so keep pimping." Nelly's definition of the phrase is fully in line with how many within the hip hop generation have come to think about pimps and pimping.

Many of the youngest of the hip hop generation were not privy to 1970s television dramas like *Starsky & Hutch* and *Kojak* or films like *The Mack* and *Superfly*, where black male pimps were staple characters. Antonio Fargas, who played Huggy Bear on *Starsky and Hutch*, may have been the most recognizable "pimp" in America during the 1970s. Some of the older cats can remember reading the fiction of Robert Beck—Iceberg Slim—whose novels *Pimp* and *Trick Baby* were required reading for wannabe playas in the '70s. As John Robinson notes in *The Guardian*, for Slim the pimp game was "seldom about violence to women. It was all about verbal persuasion . . . charm." Noted historian Robin D.G. Kelley made a similar observation in a controversial *New York Times* article about Miles Davis. In the piece Kelley suggested that the legendary jazz artist was a product of the "pimp aesthetic . . . a masculine culture that aspired to be like a pimp, that embraced the cool performative styles of the players (pronounced "playa"), the "macks," the hustlers, who not only circulated in the jazz world but whose walk and talk also drew from the well of black music." (It should be noted though that Davis *was* an abuser of women.)

Cartoonish Characters

For many within the hip hop generation, pimps were cartoonish characters in music videos like Snoop's "Doggy Dog

World," figures that Snoop, Too Short ("Pimpin' Ain't Easy") and others nostalgically paid tribute to with shoulder length perms, big-ass Cadillacs and "now-and-later" gators. Of course pimps gained new credibility this year [2003] on the strength of 50 Cent's "P.I.M.P.," which featured Snoop and a cameo by Bishop Don "Magic" Juan, the chairman of the board of the Famous Players Association, sponsors of the legendary Players Ball. Hip hop's fascination with the pimp aesthetic dates back to the release of the *Hustler's Convention* (1973), a recording from former Last Poet Jalal Nuriddin, who used the name Lightnin' Rod for the album.

Generally speaking, pimps have been some of the most nefarious characters to ever languish (it's not like they're thriving) within black communities, finding power and influence in their exploitation and often violent control of black female sexuality. But in many regards the bad reputation that pimps have endured has been a smoke screen to mask the equally nefarious exploitative habits of those within more "respectable" black institutions. Common alluded to such a reality in his song "Film Called (Pimp)," as he gives up the game telling his would-be "ho," well "F—— you then, I'm about to be a preacher." While the Chi-town native may have been shouting out fellow Chi-town playa Bishop Don "Magic" Juan, who after a religious experience in 1985, gave up the game for the pulpit, there's no small irony in the fact that the very skills that make an effective pimp, may in fact be desired and valued by men of the cloth.

Missing the Point

Such ironies are well beyond the scope of folks like Project Islamic Hope, the National Alliance for Positive Action and the National Black Anti-Defamation League, who along with Ministers Michael Pfleger and Paul Scott are calling for a national black boycott of *Pimp Juice*. According to Najee Ali of Project Islamic Hope, "We intend to chase Nelly's *Pimp Juice* out of the black community." Scott added from his Durham, N.C., base, "As black men we should be building a nation of strong black leaders, not a nation of super energized, drunk pimps." Columnist Clarence Page chimed in that "back in the prehistoric age before there was rap music or, for that matter, laptops or cell phones, my generation had such terms as 'pimp walk,' 'pimp style' or simply 'pimpin' some sucker who didn't know any better. But we never had any confusion as to where the word came from."

To Be a Pimp Is to Be Cool

To reference pimping today—whether via noun, verb or adjective—is to have it both ways: It's to tap the well of hypermasculine "cool" that's long been stereotypically associated with African-American men . . . while at the same time defusing anything potentially threatening about such a forceful pose. What could possibly be threatening about "pimping" a cellphone? Or about party-happy Nelly beaming beside his can of "Pimp Juice," or Big Snoop Dogg, shizzling his nizzles in an over-the-top Cadillac?

Baz Dresinger, Salon.com, July 2004.

Page's comments get to the heart of the controversy, as this is another example of how much distance there is between the Civil Rights old guard and the hip hop generation. Whereas the old guard can only see literal pimps, many within the hip hop generation have redefined the word to suit the needs of the post–Civil Rights era world. While the word still alludes to the practice of exploitation, it is no longer solely rooted in some archaic notion of "pimps up, ho's down." Much like the word "nigger," the word "pimp" is a "troublesome word" (as our resident niggerologist Randall Kennedy would suggest). As Nelly cogently described to Sylvester Brown, Jr. in the *St. Louis Post-Dispatch*, "What we have been able to do in hip hop is to take a negative and turn it into a positive . . . if you pimp something, that means you're getting the most out of the best of your ability."

Empowering Women

This sentiment was expressed exactly a year ago when organizers of the *Pimp Harder* fashion show at last year's Homecoming celebration at Howard University, responded to accusations that they were normalizing pathological behavior. According to organizers Jessica Lima and Megan Moore, they hoped the show would inspire Howard students to "conquer what oppresses them and become pimps in their own right." For these women the word "pimp" can even be applied to feminist sensibilities. As Moore asserts, "pimping is a state of mind . . . a movement about no longer being the victim, a movement where women do not have to take some of the crap that men dish out."

One must question the motivation of a group like Project Islamic Hope, which has been at odds with the hip hop generation since they lobbied against Tupac Shakur's nomination for an NAACP [National Association for the Advancement of Colored People] Image Award in the early 1990s. Earlier this year they called for a boycott of the television series *Platinum*, arguing that it celebrated the worst aspects of hip hop culture. I'm with my man William Jelani Cobb on this one—with all the critical issues that black folks are currently challenged by, why is so much energy being expended over trivial issues, like the name of an energy drink. One wonders where Project Islamic Hope or the National Black Anti-Defamation League were when a suspected "gay" student was beat-down in a homophobic attack in a Morehouse College bathroom last year or how come they haven't called for a boycott of R. Kelly records after his indictment on 21 charges of child pornography. Perhaps it's because said groups also understand the pimp-game and they have successfully pimped the trivial and the inane in black life so they could do their own pimp strut for the national media.

*"Ladies, the way you dress does matter.
Please, put on some decent clothes."*

Popular Culture Encourages Girls to Wear Revealing Clothing

Jared Jackson

According to Jared Jackson in the following viewpoint, sexual marketing and lewd TV programs are adversely affecting teen fashion. He asserts that many teenage girls now wear low-rider jeans that expose their midriff, and sport tattoos and navel piercings. Young men also dress provocatively, he contends. The result of this sexualization of children is an increase in sexually transmitted disease and unwanted pregnancies, Jackson argues. Jared Jackson is a frequent contributor to *Christian Courier.*

As you read, consider the following questions:

1. According to Jackson, what is society teaching young girls about how to grow into womanhood?
2. What message does the media send to young boys, according to the author?
3. According to the author, what does the Bible teach about dressing modestly?

Jared Jackson, "Belly-Button Rings and Low-Rider Jeans," www.ChristianCourier.com, June 28, 2004. Copyright © 2004 by Christian Courier Publications. Reproduced by permission.

It was once the case that the only time "love-handles" were exposed in public was when an overweight plumber was struggling to repair the faucet (no offense to plumbers intended).

Low-Rider Jeans and Belly-Button Rings

These days, every other teen-age girl at the mall is wearing her favorite pair of "I wear a size 8, but the 6's fit so tight, I went ahead and got the 4's" low-rider jeans that let her wiggle around in pride, showing off her new tattoo just above the caboose along with the belly-button ring she bought with last week's allowance.

From early on, our society teaches the feminine child that body glitter and exposed cleavage are the rites of passage that will carry her to the status of "cosmopolitan womanhood." From the time they can fantasize with the Barbie doll that has become progressively more lumpy over the years, to the day she can pick up the latest "sophisticated" women's magazines, our daughters are slowly being pressed into a mold of destruction and ruin.

Pushing Adult Styles on Children

Even underwear that only a few years ago was considered "for adults only" is now in vogue for innocent girls at the tenderest age. Recently, the infamous Abercrombie & Fitch porn and clothing store began testing the limits by peddling a line of thong underwear for girls as young as 10 or 12 years old garnished with pictures of cherries, and suggestive words like "kiss me," "wink wink," and "eye candy." Despite the public outcry, the hustlers know that they can pull back, wait a while, then steam on ahead.

When your daughter is walking around with "kiss me" stamped on her "derriere," what kind of message do you think is being advertised?

The young men in our culture are no less targets of the allure of "glamorous" living. Almost every break in any given televised sports event is peppered with seductive women and carefree young men promoting one prevailing hedonistic message. The adolescent men walk around with their underwear hanging out all over the place, with perhaps something that might be called a shirt. And when mom or dad complain about their son's behavior, the boys reaffirm their independence and personal sovereignty—then ask for twenty bucks and the car keys.

The Devastating Fallout

What is the result of this permeation of sexual marketing and anemic parenting? The fallout is devastating.

Every year, some 12 million Americans contract a sexually transmitted disease; 63% are less than 25 years old.

Every year, nearly 1 million girls between the ages of 15–19 become pregnant; approximately a quarter million of these end their pregnancy by aborting the baby.

The teen mother who keeps the baby will most likely not complete high school, and become a permanent dependent of her parents. Her child will probably have poorer health, fall behind in school, and is more likely to become the victim of abuse and neglect. The father is long gone on to greener pastures—frequently without a thought of the fruit of their sinful, irresponsible behavior. The new mom and her parents are left with heartache and stress, and a child that desperately needs a family as God planned for her.

There may be exceptions to the bleak picture painted above. Still, they are exceptions.

In the not-too-distant past, it was the case that if you went to a public amusement park, or even to the local shopping mall, you would expect to see the fashion sense of worldliness walking around.

Now, however, it is increasingly the case that the young women and men in the Lord's church are not only wearing immodest apparel with abandon, but they are even arriving to worship the Lord of heaven and earth dressed so inappropriately. Young ladies, with exposed cleavage and tight, revealing clothes sit beside disheveled young men wearing wrinkled T-shirts and scruffy sweatpants. Occasionally, they even have the nerve to "make-out" on the church parking lot.

Preachers and Elders Must Get Involved

Preachers and elders need to lovingly, yet firmly, address this type of behavior. We ought not be intimidated by permissive

The Difference Between Cute and Provocative

As a service to any woman who is confused by the difference between 'cute' and provocative as regards women's clothing, this may help. What you often call cute or attractive, men see only as a sexual come-on. If you wish to dress for sex, you should be entirely free to do so. But if you want love and attention, you have to know the difference between dressing for sex and dressing to be cute and attractive. The more skin men see, the more they think sex, not love. And that includes guys your age, your male teachers, your clergyman, your mailman, and the old man next door.

Dennis Prager, Townhall.com, February 17, 2004.

---

parents who resist biblical teaching when it is applied to their precious offspring. Lessons from the pulpit are important. But so is courageous, personal counseling.

Parents, especially fathers, you need to exercise the authority and discipline *the* Father has bestowed upon you. If your children are dressed for success in Satan's cause, it is your fault. If they live in your house, take a stand. They may kick and scream, but it's up to you to set the standard in your household.

Moms, please don't make your daughter the object of your vicarious teenage rebellion. Teach your tender offspring the value of purity and honor. The greatest gift you can give her is the self-respect of not needing to rely upon her curls and curves to achieve the great milestones in life. Actively teach her that she can instead rely upon the majesty of her heavenly Father (1 Pet. 2:9), the mind of Christ (Phil. 2:5), and the humility of Mary (Lk. 1:38). Those traits will last much longer, even into eternity.

Young men, tuck in your shirts and show some dignity. Act like Timothy, not like p-Daddy diddly doo or whoever is the big-shot rapper of the day (Dude, that means like, read 1 & 2 Timothy!). A good dose of the Proverbs are prescribed as well.

The Way You Dress Matters

Ladies, the way you dress does matter. Please, put on some decent clothes. You may not contract an STD or get pregnant, but avoiding those results are pretty good reasons to live pure and wholesome lives.

If those aren't good enough reasons, at least dress modestly for the sake of those around you. There are men who will be weakened by your display. And if you don't care about them, at least have the dignity and self-respect to not advertise yourself as a cheap sex object.

Ultimately, you ought to comport yourself as the temple of the Holy Spirit, for such you are (1 Cor. 6:19). Instead of trying to turn the heads, try turning the hearts with a beauty of holiness and depth of character possessed by the great women in the Bible.

"And be not fashioned according to this world: but be ye transformed by the renewing of your mind, that ye may prove what is the good and acceptable and perfect will of God" (Rom. 12:2).

> "Many thought the world would end when
> women started to wear pants and left the
> traditional strait-laced skirts in the closet."

Revealing Teen Fashions Do Not Harm Children

Rhonda Hollen

Prudish adults should not criticize or legislate against teen fashions they think sexualize children, Rhonda Hollen contends in the following viewpoint. She grants that pop stars Britney Spears and Christina Aguilera have inspired girls to wear low-rise jeans that expose their midriffs, but she argues that such attire is merely a fashion statement, not a sign of social degradation. Rhonda Hollen is a student editor at the Louisiana State University newspaper *Tiger Weekly*.

As you read, consider the following questions:
1. According to the author, how do normal, educated people react to the sight of low-rise pants?
2. What punishment would the failed legislation against low-rise pants have imposed, according to Hollen?
3. According to the author, what is the primary complaint about low-rise pants?

Rhonda Hollen, "Just 'Butt Out' of Our Closets, Please," *Tiger Weekly*, 2004. Copyright © 2004 by University Media Group. Reproduced by permission.

Highway workers, plumbers and even the guy washing his car this weekend have an issue with their exterior, or let's just say "junk in the trunk." The dilemma, or rather jokingly, eyeful, is that they're baring exteriors that might not appreciate feeling the effects of the outside environment. Showing larger versions of less than rosy cheeks didn't start yesterday, and I do believe that until their jobs cease to be, the rough and ready laborers will feel pride in tilling the cement and lifting up their precious bottoms. We all know there are other cracks than those on local roads. Most normal, life educated people know this and just drive on.

Thanks to pioneers like Christina Aguilera, Britney Spears and "pardon my buttocks Construction Joe," low-slung jeans tingle the thighs of many young adults. One lawmaker, however, isn't following the hipster cult by registering a bill that would ban youth from wearing pants below the waist [the bill did not pass].

Trying to Outlaw Revealing Clothes

Rep. Derrick Shepherd from Jefferson Parish, the observant lawmaker that he is, is tired of seeing boxer shorts and G-strings over the low-slung belt lines of teenagers. Well, I'm tired of political men like Shepherd, who instead of filing a monumental bill that would forever change the face of a community and promote sincere positive acts for all law-abiding, respective citizens, feel free to act like parents of children they have never held a conversation with. They're wasting their time and mine by complaining about a seemingly brick wall. Mr. Shepherd needs to put down the binoculars and go back to work!

The bill would punish those following the popular fashion trend with a fine as expensive as $500. But wait—there's more. Not only could an impressionable and sensitive 13-year-old girl wearing low-riding jeans and tons of flavored lip gloss be faced with more financial trouble than she imagined in 2nd hour PE class, but also with a six-month prison sentence. Now, isn't that a pretty picture. Because Mr. Shepherd feels like her parents aren't doing their job by stopping their daughter on the way out the door because she is wearing today's fashion and showing some skin, she will have a record.

The correlation between low-slung jeans and the teenage generation has been scrutinized for promoting a negative, premature sense of fashion maturity and questionable sexiness.

Healthy Confidence

Condemning any women for wearing revealing clothes fosters low self-esteem among all women and perpetuates the existence of eating disorders. Wearing tight or minimal clothing demonstrates healthy confidence. Feminists need to worry much more about the girl who is ashamed to bare her stomach than the one with the visible belly button piercing.

Kimberly Liu, *The Cavalier Daily*, April 26, 2002.

I still remember a JC Penny ad featuring a young girl admiring her crop top and low-rise jeans outfit when her mother came into the room, and after saying she couldn't go to school like that, inched her jeans down lower about another inch, saying "There, that's better." JC Penny pulled the ad off of the airways, but without a doubt, the younger generation hasn't stopped gazing at the apparel on clothes racks and handing over millions of dollars to the fashion industry yearly.

Prudish Adults Attacking Fashion

Many thought the world would end when women started to wear pants and left the traditional strait-laced skirts in the closet. Prudish adults who spend their time attacking the younger generation need to realize that we are in the midst of a fashion statement, not a social revolution.

Just because you have a problem with how someone dresses doesn't justify suggesting laws which target a certain group. I sometimes see others wearing clothing that I wouldn't be caught dead in, but I realize that they have the right to wear what they want. That's my end, Mr. Shepherd.

"It's not 'the American way' for broadcasters to shovel smut out of the television set and then say no one is allowed to define obscenity as obscene."

The Federal Communications Commission Should Crack Down on TV Obscenity

L. Brent Bozell III

Despite media protests to the contrary, the Federal Communications Commission is correct to enforce indecency regulations, according to L. Brent Bozell III in the following viewpoint. Bozell claims that the FCC's crackdown on the use of obscenity in TV programs does not violate the First Amendment to the U.S. Constitution. L. Brent Bozell III is founder and president of the Media Research Center, a conservative organization that monitors and criticizes the media for offensive content.

As you read, consider the following questions:

1. According to Bozell, why are some free-speech advocates hypocritical?
2. What is the difference between planned and unplanned broadcasts of indecency, according to the media?
3. According to the author, what is the media's defense for its broadcast of obscene language?

L. Brent Bozell III, "The Pro-Indecency Lobby," www.mediaresearch.org, April 23, 2004. Copyright © 2004 by Creators Syndicate, Inc. Reproduced by permission.

The new seriousness at the Federal Communications Commission [FCC] toward basic, unmissable profanity on broadcast television and radio is beginning to draw great protest from the proponents of profanity and indecency. They have unfurled the banner of the First Amendment and utter the usual buzzwords and mantras: free speech, censorship, chilling effect. Then there's a new one: "creative integrity."

This last one comes from NBC president Robert Wright, who wrote a passionate editorial in the *Wall Street Journal* claiming the TV elite are the titans of "creative integrity," and must not be protested. "Ultimately, we have much less to fear from obscene, indecent or profane content than we do from an overzealous government willing to limit First Amendment protections and censor creative free expression. That would be indecent," Wright insisted.

Protesting Smut Is Indecent?

It's an argument Howard Stern would love: it's not smut that is indecent, it's protesting smut that's indecent! It's like saying cigarettes don't kill people, the anti-tobacco lobby does.

Wright and other activists are now condemning the FCC for defining NBC's airing of the F-word during the Golden Globe Awards as obscene. Apparently, the F-word is the very height of "creative integrity." I wonder if Robert Wright taught his own children that profanity is creative, and laced with integrity.

NBC filed its own brief of protest at the FCC: The other, more publicized brief—covered with headlines like "Hollywood Fights Back"—can be found at the Web site of People for the American Way. It is signed by Fox Entertainment, Viacom (CBS, MTV, etc.), the American Civil Liberties Union [ACLU], several broadcasting lobby groups, the magician duo Penn & Teller, and the potty-mouthed bisexual comic Margaret Cho.

This coalition is not interested in the broader cause of free speech—you will not see Margaret Cho or Penn & Teller speaking out for the right of high school children to pray at the flag pole, or the right of a graduation speaker to credit Jesus as a positive influence in his or her life. (In fact, the ACLU is an aggressive litigant against this form of "offensive speech.") This brief is an overt effort to make America's air-waves safe for the F-word. It warns the FCC's Golden Globes ruling that "the isolated use of an unplanned and unscripted expletive is both 'indecent' and 'profane' represents an un-constitutional expansion of the government's intrusion into broadcast content."

Protecting Children

As a member of the federal agency responsible for prosecut-ing those who peddle indecent broadcast programming, I can assure all Americans that this [Federal Communications] Commission will continue to protect children and respond to the public's concerns. Under our authority, and consistent with the First Amendment, we will continue to vigorously enforce our indecency rules. . . . Protecting children and giv-ing parents the tools to restrict inappropriate programming from unexpectedly invading our family rooms requires ac-tion on all fronts. The effort begins with the Commission.

Michael K. Powell, testimony before the U.S. Senate Committee on Com-merce, Science, and Transportation, February 11, 2004.

Don't they know people start giggling when they try to say the F-word is not profane because it was "unplanned"? Or that it's not indecent if it was an "adverbial intensifier" that did not describe "sexual or excretory activities"? This is where the public starts rolling its eyes about lawyers trying to manipu-late language into meaning nothing, or anything at all.

This ambitiously disingenuous brief is authored by lawyer Robert Corn-Revere, who represented Playboy Entertain-ment Group before the Supreme Court in 1996. Who is pay-ing him for his lobbying effort this time? His speech isn't so free-flowing on that question. *The New York Times* reported Corn-Revere "would not say which organization initially en-gaged him to pursue the petition." He's also presently work-ing for Florida entrepreneur Stuart Lawley, who's attempting to prevent Congress from requiring an "xxx" domain code for Internet porn peddlers.

Pro-Indecency Lobbyists

When he sat beside this writer in a Congressional hearing in January [2004], Corn-Revere acknowledged he "actively represented" clients in the entertainment business, but insisted "my testimony represents my personal views, and should not necessarily be attributed to my clients." That's at the very least misleading, since his personal views seem to be indistinguishable from his sleaze-merchandising clients.

Every lame complaint is tossed into the basket here. The Hollywood pro-indecency brief complains that the FCC ruling reflects "arbitrary" regulation, since the commission overruled its so-called "Enforcement Bureau" on its finding that NBC's F-word was not profane. How dare the FCC's commissioners override their staff!

The pro-indecency brief also suggests it is intolerable that the FCC "no longer requires that complaints be substantiated, and that, in some cases, no complaint need be filed at all." Is anyone willing to suggest that the Bono outburst [when he used an obscene word during an awards show broadcast] on NBC *never happened?* What next, Hollywood? That the FCC can't really substantiate that Madonna and Britney Spears kissed on MTV? That it's uncertain if the Super Bowl half-time show fiasco[1] occurred?

Lobbies like People for the American Way ought to know that it's not "the American way" to win political arguments without a debate. It's not "the American way" for broadcasters to shovel smut out of the television set and then say no one is allowed to define obscenity as obscene—or complain. The American way means you have to persuade the public on the merits of your case, and it doesn't look good to people when you use every euphemism and piece of legalistic mumbo-jumbo to insist that the F-word is somehow not profane.

---

1. During the 2004 Super Bowl halftime show, singer Janet Jackson's breast was exposed and seen by millions on live TV.

"The puritanical weed appears to be coming back into full bloom."

The Federal Communications Commission Should Not Crack Down on TV Obscenity

Doug Casey

In the following viewpoint Doug Casey argues that the Federal Communications Commission (FCC) is wrong to crack down on TV obscenity. Judging the appropriateness of television content should be left to the viewers, who will stop watching if offended by certain content, he maintains. In Casey's opinion, the FCC is simply a vehicle through which puritanical Americans can control what TV programs others watch. Doug Casey is a writer, publisher, and professional investor. He is also the author of *Crisis Investing*.

As you read, consider the following questions:
1. According to Casey, what was the result of the FCC's pressure on media conglomerate Clear Channel?
2. How has the FCC slowed the spread of new media technologies, in the author's view?
3. According to the author, how did the Puritans deal with religious dissent?

Doug Casey, "The New Puritans," www.WorldNetDaily.com, June 10, 2004. Copyright © 2004 by WorldNetDaily.com. Reproduced by permission.

Among the earliest pioneers in this country were the Puritans of the Massachusetts Bay Colony, who set out to create a theocracy—a Bible-thumping commonwealth as it were.

In fact, until as late as 1664, citizenship in the new colony was restricted to church members, and religious dissent was not tolerated. (The nation's earliest religious dissenters, most notably Anne Hutchinson and Roger Williams, were actually banished from the colony.)

The seeds sown by those Puritans have persisted through American history, albeit with the normal ebb and flow of society. The roaring '20s and psychedelic '60s are, to my way of thinking, more representative of why America is great than the societies of the Pilgrims and the Puritans.

The New Puritans

The puritanical weed appears to be coming back into full bloom, what with the smirking chimp and the thought-police cracking down on "immorality" in all its many guises. Taking the ball from Janet Jackson's [2004] Super Bowl breast exposure, the Federal Communications Commission [FCC] is running down the field knocking over anyone that it, in its wisdom, considers to be eroding the public morality.

Like scores of millions of other Americans (and I believe even more Chinese, but that's another story) I, too, watched the Super Bowl in January. It was a hell of a game. When Janet's breast made its appearance, I didn't really know what to make of it, but, as a fan of much in popular culture, from "South Park" to Madonna videos, I simply assumed it was part of the show.

It must be an indicator of how open-minded I am, or easily amused, or jaded, or maybe just out of touch with the strain of Puritanism that continues to flow in the veins of *Boobus americanus*, that I gave it no more thought. Until apparently scandalized reporters filled the media with reports of how outraged the country was. That got my attention a lot more than Justin and Janet.

I've come to accept the fact that my political, economic, religious, military, ethical, social and—need I add—investment views, are somewhat out of the norm in the United States. But I still shake my head in disbelief (even though, intellectually, I suspect it's true) that people actually become so exercised over things of this nature.

The Self-Righteous FCC

Then the self-righteous bluenoses at the FCC weighed in with threats to fine CBS, and possibly its executives, millions of dollars. They theoretically have the right to revoke CBS's broadcast licenses, effectively bankrupting the entity.

Since that incident, the FCC has pressured Clear Channel to drop, among others, [shock jock] Howard Stern, the poster child for "bad" media.

An Attack on Our Personal Freedom

It amazes me to read how people like Adolph Hitler and Joseph McCarthy were able to rise to power. It happened when good people stood by and did nothing. I fear that we are on the verge of another puritanical and politically motivated attack on our personal freedoms.

Rusty White, *Entertainment Insiders*, March 8, 2004.

But I always try to look at the bright side. Now that the FCC has crawled out from under its rock, in time more people will begin to take a closer look at this singularly useless corner of bureaucracy. Howard Stern, for one, is using his widely heard bully pulpit to fight back against the agency, which he accuses of going after him because of his outspoken views on Baby Bush [George W. Bush] and not for his supposed outrages against society.

It is worth noting that since Clear Channel caved in to the pressure, Stern's ratings have gone up to where he has regained the top slot in New York, Los Angeles and Chicago, the three biggest radio markets in the United States.

It's not as if the agency hasn't been very good to me, and *International Speculator* subscribers. In the early '80s, when the FCC was having lotteries to assign frequencies for cellular telephones, among numerous other technologies, I urged readers to apply for the giveaways. I personally won several million dollars on them and know that some subscribers did even better.

The FCC Is Unproductive

Hey, the redistribution of wealth is actually the main purpose of government. It's just that the FCC never does anything productive, unless it usurps that function from the market. Certainly things like assigning frequencies, call letters and such are market functions, as are "decency standards"—if a broadcaster doesn't give the public what it wants, it won't get advertisers and/or subscribers, and will put itself out of business.

What the FCC's 2,000 employees mainly do, at a direct cost of $280 million a year—and an indirect cost that must be many billions—is protect the politically well-connected, mainly by slowing the spread of technology. Examples?

- The FCC (aided and abetted by local regulators) delayed cable TV for years at the urging of traditional broadcasters.
- It's solely responsible for keeping telephone costs way up and innovation way down by protecting AT&T's monopoly for decades before reality finally overcame it.
- Cellular phones were delayed for years.

The FCC is basically a vehicle for restricting entry of newcomers into the electronic media, much to the benefit of those who have already jumped over the expensive hurdles required to get its licenses.

The whole episode that started this latest wave of attempted control by the latter-day Puritans is disgusting, from Janet's phony claim that it was an "accident," to the FCC's grandstanding, to talk of putting in five-second delays on live performances that may serve to outrage the *booboisie*.

What might the 200 million mainland Chinese watchers have thought of the Super Bowl incident? My guess is: "What a great, free, easygoing country America is! We should make China more like it!" If only they knew the rest of the story.

Periodical Bibliography

The following articles have been selected to supplement the diverse views presented in this chapter.

Kathleen O. Abernathy — Testimony before the U.S. Senate Committee on Commerce, Science, and Transportation, February 11, 2004.

L. Brent Bozell III — "Is There a Broadcast Standard?" November 27, 2002. www.Parentstv.org.

Doug Casey — "The New Puritans," June 10, 2004. www. worldnetdaily.com.

Duewa Frazier — "MCs—No More Video Hoes," *Essence*, August 2004.

Orrin Hatch — Statement before the Senate Judiciary Committee during hearing on Indecent Exposure: Oversight of DOJ's Efforts to Protect Pornography's Victims, October 15, 2003.

Robert Ito — "Cup of Plenty," *Los Angeles Magazine*, May 2004.

Helen Lee — "Can Female Listeners Tame Shock Jocks?" *Insight on the News*, April 13, 2004.

Modern Brewery Age — "Not Just for Pimps Anymore—Pimp Juice," July 21, 2003.

Kevin Forest Moreau — "The Passion of Howard Stern," February 27, 2004. www.shakingthrough.net.

Michael K. Powell — Testimony before the U.S. Senate Committee on Commerce, Science, and Transportation, February 11, 2004.

Santa Cruz Sentinel — "Overreaction Is Offensive: Government Should Not Decide What Adults Can or Cannot See on TV," February 13, 2004.

Cal Thomas — "Must-Sleaze TV?" May 8, 2001. www. townhall.com.

Matt Welch — "Fair-Weather Friends: When Journalists Desert from Free-Speech Battles," *Reason*, June 2004.

Rusty White — "Howard Stern and the New McCarthyism," March 8, 2004. www.einsiders.com.

CHAPTER 3

Is Popular Culture Too Violent?

Chapter Preface

The controversy surrounding violence in popular culture is intense but not new. Indeed, throughout history, violence has been a staple of popular culture, prompting debate about whether depictions of violence promote real-world violence.

Four thousand years ago, the ancient Egyptians watched plays depicting the murder of the god Osiris. According to some accounts written at that time, the violent dramas led to copycat killings. Violent dramas were debated in ancient Greece, as well. Plato, in his *Republic*, argued that explicit poems and bedtime stories should not be recited because they could implant immoral ideas in children's minds. His pupil Aristotle, however, disagreed. He believed that the presentation of tragedies helped viewers to rid themselves of fears and anxieties. He used the term *katharsis* (catharsis) to describe the experience.

In ancient Rome, violent dramas such as the Greeks enjoyed would be considered tame; the violent entertainment of the day in Rome was not staged, but real. The Romans built amphitheaters to stage various types of violent contests. The Latin word for arena, *harena*, means sand, which covered the ground of the amphitheater to soak up the blood that resulted from gladiator combat and other violent entertainments, in which warriors fought to the death and men engaged in deadly battles with wild animals such as lions. Saint Augustine complained at the time that society was "drunk with the fascination of bloodshed."

In the sixteenth century, Shakespeare's tragedies such as *Hamlet* and *Macbeth* were extremely popular and extremely bloody. Critics bemoaned the violent content of some of Shakespeare's plays. About *Hamlet*, for example, in which all the main characters die through murder or suicide, the French writer Voltaire wrote that "there is quarrelling, fighting, killing—one would imagine this piece to be the work of a drunken savage."

By the beginning of the twentieth century, the new medium of motion pictures quickly became a dominant force in entertainment, and film violence soon became a concern. In response to complaints about sexual and violent content in early films, the Production Code was adopted by the movie industry in March 1930. The code specified that "the technique of murder must be presented in a way that will not inspire imitation" and that "brutal killings are not to be presented in detail." Of greatest concern was the impact of violent images on children, especially in light of the popularity of the new gangster movie genre. In 1933 the Payne Fund sponsored a study on the impact of violent films on children. It concluded that children were "unmarked slates" that needed protection from violent imagery in movies.

During World War II, the Office of War Information was responsible for ensuring that Hollywood studios supported the war. The government was concerned about depictions of war that were too graphic for fear that they would undermine the war effort. As a result, in the early years of the war, the horrors of combat were glossed over in movies. However, toward the end of the war, audiences began to demand more realistic depictions of violence that were consistent with the experiences of returning veterans.

After the war and the breakup of the studio system in 1948, even more graphically violent movies began to emerge, especially those in the film noir genre such as *Kiss Me Deadly*, which came out in 1950. By the late 1950s rebellious directors such as Otto Preminger began to release their films without the Production Code seal of approval and experienced great success. Examples are *The Man with the Golden Arm* (1955) and *Anatomy of a Murder* (1959). By 1967 changing societal standards had rendered the Production Code obsolete, and it was abandoned. The movie rating system was established the following year.

In the 1960s and 1970s new creative freedom combined with superior special effects technology made possible the release of the most blood-soaked films made to date: *Bonnie and Clyde* (1967), *The Wild Bunch* (1969), and *Straw Dogs* (1972), which featured graphic depictions of rape and murder.

In the following viewpoints some authors criticize today's popular culture for its violent content while others defend the artists' right to freedom of expression. It appears that the same arguments about violent entertainment from thousands of years ago will undoubtedly continue well into the future.

> *"There is absolutely no doubt that those who are heavy viewers of [media] violence demonstrate increased acceptance of aggressive attitudes and increased aggressive behavior."*

Media Violence Promotes Violent Behavior

Ed Donnerstein

In the following viewpoint Ed Donnerstein argues that although media violence may not be the most important contributor to violent behavior, it has been proven to have an adverse impact on viewers. If the violence is depicted in a glamorous, sanitized, or routine manner, as it frequently is on television and in movies, it sends the message that violence is a desirable way to solve problems, he contends. Ed Donnerstein is dean of the College of Social and Behavioral Sciences at the University of Arizona.

As you read, consider the following questions:
1. What did the office of the surgeon general of the United States conclude about media violence?
2. What role should parents play in preventing the influence of violence in the media, according to Donnerstein?
3. According to the author, what actions should the mass media take to counter the aggressive behavior inspired by their violent content?

Ed Donnerstein, "Violence in Media," *Arizona Alumnus*, Fall 2004. Copyright © 2004 by Ed Donnerstein. Reproduced by permission.

I was taken aback when congressional hearings and an inordinate amount of media coverage were devoted to the issue of indecency on television after the [2004] Janet Jackson Super Bowl incident. Our government "media regulators" demonstrated that they were more concerned about the influence of an exposed breast on "innocent children" than the one area we know the most about—exposure to violence in the media.

The relationship between exposure to media violence and aggressive behavior has been an ongoing focus of inquiry by academic researchers and major health organizations for years. In particular, a recent report on youth violence from the Office of the Surgeon General of the United States found strong evidence that exposure to violence in the media is one of a number of risk factors that can increase children's "aggressive behavior" in the short term, and concluded that there should be sustained efforts to curb the adverse effects of media violence on youths.

There is universal agreement that many social factors contribute to violent behavior in society including gangs, drugs, guns, poverty, and racism. Nevertheless, there has always been the realization that mass media also contributes to aggressive behavior.

There is no single cause of violent behavior, and media violence is not the most important contributor. But there is clear evidence that exposure to media violence does contribute to aggressive behavior in viewers.

Amount of Exposure

How much violence are children being exposed to? Several studies over the last three decades have been conducted to systematically assess the prevalence of violence on American television. The largest and most rigorous of these was the National Television Violence Study, which examined the amount and context of violence on American television for three consecutive years. The results revealed that 61 percent of programs on television contain some violence.

Of greater concern is the context or way in which this violence was presented. Most aggression on television is glamorized. Nearly half of the violent interactions involve perpetrators who have some attractive qualities worthy of emulation, particularly for children. Furthermore, nearly 75 percent of all violent scenes featured no immediate punishment or condemnation for violence. And almost 45 percent of the programs feature "bad" characters that are never or rarely punished for their aggressive actions.

In addition, much of the violence on television is sanitized. More than half the violent interactions featured no pain or harm to victims. Even if harm was present, almost a third was presented in an unrealistic fashion with the greatest prevalence of unrealistic harm appearing in children's programming. And more disturbing, 25 percent of all violent behaviors involved the use of a gun.

Exposure Affects the Viewer

Does all this violence do anything to the viewer? The overwhelming evidence says, "yes."

There is absolutely no doubt that those who are heavy viewers of this violence demonstrate increased acceptance of aggressive attitudes and increased aggressive behavior. These aggressive habits learned early in life form the foundation for later behavior.

In addition to increasing violent behaviors toward others, viewing violence in the media changes attitudes and behaviors toward violence in two other significant ways.

First, prolonged viewing of media violence can lead to emotional desensitization toward real-world violence and the victims of violence, which can result in callous attitudes toward aggression directed at others and a decreased likelihood to take action on behalf of the victim when violence occurs.

Second, viewing violence can increase fear of becoming a victim of violence, with a resultant increase in self-protective behaviors and increased mistrust of others.

We should not be surprised at these negative consequences because one of the major functions of the mass media is to influence viewers.

Not All Violence Is Equal

Of course, not all violent portrayals are equal with regard to the risk they might pose. The portrayal of violence need not lead to aggressive attitudes and behaviors if the consequences and harms of violence are made clear. But if violence is glamorized, sanitized, or made to seem routine, as it often is, then the message is that it is an acceptable, and perhaps even desirable, course of action.

Ramirez. © 2000 by Copley News Service. Reproduced by permission.

I, like others, am certain that there are potential harmful influences of exposure to specific media depictions. But there are a number of potential solutions to these concerns.

Professionals must take a more active role in reducing the impact of violent media.

We can reduce some of the impact of media violence by "empowering" parents in their roles as monitors of children's media viewing (including the Internet).

Media literacy and critical viewing skills, taught as part of school curriculum, are strong intervention strategies toward mitigating the impact of violent media.

The mass media itself needs to be part of the solution. For example, professionally produced movies about violence, that are also designed to be entertaining, have great potential for informing the public and, under some conditions, might even change antisocial attitudes about violence.

I know that violence in the mass media contributes to a number of antisocial attitudes and behaviors in children and adolescents. Even though I realize that the mass media is but one factor, I hope its impact can be mitigated and/or controlled with reasonable insight.

Today, the average viewer has access to hundreds of channels including pay per view, video on demand, and other new digital technologies, which have drastically changed the types of media we can view in our own homes. And, of course, the Internet, for many, has taken over the function of traditional television.

I remember our family's first television. It had a circular screen and showed us the world in black and white. I was lucky because the set of "rabbit ears" we had brought in two stations. We had few choices and certainly spent few hours in front of the "tube."

The world has changed and so must we. The media, parents, and our educational system should all shoulder the responsibility to prevent the antisocial effects of exposure to media violence.

> "[Media violence has] helped hundreds of
> people for every one it's hurt."

Media Violence Promotes Healthy Behavior

Gerard Jones

Gerard Jones argues in the following viewpoint that aggression is a natural human trait and that violent entertainment can provide a way for children to channel their aggression in healthy ways. In addition, he claims that research shows that even the most violent pop culture entertainment can help children become more sure of themselves. Gerard Jones is the author, with Lynn Ponton, of *Killing Monsters: Why Children Need Fantasy, Super Heroes, and Make-Believe Violence.*

As you read, consider the following questions:

1. According to Jones, how was the title character in the comic *The Hulk* helpful to him as he grew up?
2. How was Emily helped by pop culture, according to Jones?
3. According to the author, why is it dangerous to shield children from violent entertainment?

Gerard Jones, "Violent Media Is Good for Kids," *Mother Jones*, June 28, 2000. Copyright © 2000 by the Foundation for National Progress. Reproduced by permission.

At 13, I was alone and afraid. Taught by my well-meaning, progressive, English-teacher parents that violence was wrong, that rage was something to be overcome and cooperation was always better than conflict, I suffocated my deepest fears and desires under a nice-boy persona. Placed in a small, experimental school that was wrong for me, afraid to join my peers in their bumptious rush into adolescent boyhood, I withdrew into passivity and loneliness. My parents, not trusting the violent world of the late 1960s, built a wall between me and the crudest elements of American pop culture.

A Fantasy Self

Then the Incredible Hulk smashed through it.

One of my mother's students convinced her that Marvel Comics, despite their apparent juvenility and violence, were in fact devoted to lofty messages of pacifism and tolerance. My mother borrowed some, thinking they'd be good for me. And so they were. But not because they preached lofty messages of benevolence. They were good for me because they were juvenile. And violent.

The character who caught me, and freed me, was the Hulk: overgendered and undersocialized, half-naked and half-witted, raging against a frightened world that misunderstood and persecuted him. Suddenly I had a fantasy self to carry my stifled rage and buried desire for power. I had a fantasy self who was a self: unafraid of his desires and the world's disapproval, unhesitating and effective in action. "Puny boy follow Hulk!" roared my fantasy self, and I followed.

I followed him to new friends—other sensitive geeks chasing their own inner brutes—and I followed him to the arrogant, self-exposing, self-assertive, superheroic decision to become a writer. Eventually, I left him behind, followed more sophisticated heroes, and finally my own lead along a twisting path to a career and an identity. In my 30s, I found myself writing action movies and comic books. I wrote some Hulk stories, and met the geek-geniuses who created him. I saw my own creations turned into action figures, cartoons, and computer games. I talked to the kids who read my stories. Across generations, genders, and ethnicities I kept seeing the same story: people pulling themselves out of emotional traps by immersing themselves in violent stories. People integrating the scariest, most fervently denied fragments of their psyches into fuller senses of selfhood through fantasies of superhuman combat and destruction.

Defeating Fear

I have watched my son living the same story—transforming himself into a bloodthirsty dinosaur to embolden himself for the plunge into preschool, a Power Ranger to muscle through a social competition in kindergarten. In the first grade, his friends started climbing a tree at school. But he was afraid: of falling, of the centipedes crawling on the trunk, of sharp branches, of his friends' derision. I took my cue from his own fantasies and read him old Tarzan comics, rich in combat and bright with flashing knives. For two weeks he lived in them. Then he put them aside. And he climbed the tree.

But all the while, especially in the wake of the recent burst of school shootings, I heard pop psychologists insisting that violent stories are harmful to kids, heard teachers begging parents to keep their kids away from "junk culture," heard a guilt-stricken friend with a son who loved Pokémon lament, "I've turned into the bad mom who lets her kid eat sugary cereal and watch cartoons!"

That's when I started the research.

Violent Entertainment Is Necessary

"Fear, greed, power-hunger, rage: these are aspects of our selves that we try not to experience in our lives but often want, even need, to experience vicariously through stories of others," writes Melanie Moore, Ph.D., a psychologist who works with urban teens. "Children need violent entertainment in order to explore the inescapable feelings that they've been taught to deny, and to reintegrate those feelings into a more whole, more complex, more resilient selfhood."

Moore consults to public schools and local governments, and is also raising a daughter. For the past three years she and I have been studying the ways in which children use violent stories to meet their emotional and developmental needs—and the ways in which adults can help them use those stories healthily. With her help I developed Power Play, a program for helping young people improve their self-knowledge and sense of potency through heroic, combative storytelling.

A Vital Part of a Child's Development

Despite accepted interpretations of scientific studies and anecdotal evidence on the subject, there is no sound scientific evidence to indicate that exposure to violent fantasy is unhealthy; indeed, healthy engagement with adventurous, heroic, and even violent entertainment may well be a positive, vital part of a child's development.

Max Etchemendy, Free Thought Online, November 19, 2002.

We've found that every aspect of even the trashiest pop-culture story can have its own developmental function. Pretending to have superhuman powers helps children conquer the feelings of powerlessness that inevitably come with being so young and small. The dual-identity concept at the heart of many superhero stories helps kids negotiate the conflicts between the inner self and the public self as they work through the early stages of socialization. Identification with a rebellious, even destructive, hero helps children learn to push back against a modern culture that cultivates fear and teaches dependency.

Creative Violence

At its most fundamental level, what we call "creative violence" —head-bonking cartoons, bloody videogames, playground karate, toy guns—gives children a tool to master their rage. Children will feel rage. Even the sweetest and most civilized of them, even those whose parents read the better class of literary magazines, will feel rage. The world is uncontrollable and incomprehensible; mastering it is a terrifying, enraging task. Rage can be an energizing emotion, a shot of courage to push us to resist greater threats, take more control, than we ever thought we could. But rage is also the emotion our culture distrusts the most. Most of us are taught early on to fear our own. Through immersion in imaginary combat and identification with a violent protagonist, children engage the rage they've stifled, come to fear it less, and become more capable of utilizing it against life's challenges.

I knew one little girl who went around exploding with fantasies so violent that other moms would draw her mother aside to whisper, "I think you should know something about Emily. . . ." Her parents were separating, and she was small, an only child, a tomboy at an age when her classmates were dividing sharply along gender lines. On the playground she acted out "Sailor Moon" fights, and in the classroom she wrote stories about people being stabbed with knives. The more adults tried to control her stories, the more she acted out the roles of her angry heroes: breaking rules, testing limits, roaring threats.

Then her mother and I started helping her tell her stories. She wrote them, performed them, drew them like comics: sometimes bloody, sometimes tender, always blending the images of pop culture with her own most private fantasies. She came out of it just as fiery and strong, but more self-controlled and socially competent: a leader among her peers, the one student in her class who could truly pull boys and girls together.

I worked with an older girl, a middle-class "nice girl," who held herself together through a chaotic family situation and a tumultuous adolescence with gangsta rap. In the mythologized street violence of Ice T, the rage and strutting of his music and lyrics, she found a theater of the mind in which she could be powerful, ruthless, invulnerable. She avoided the heavy drug use that sank many of her peers, and flowered in college as a writer and political activist.

Media Violence Helps More than It Hurts

I'm not going to argue that violent entertainment is harmless. I think it has helped inspire some people to real-life violence. I am going to argue that it's helped hundreds of people for every one it's hurt, and that it can help far more if we learn to use it well. I am going to argue that our fear of "youth violence" isn't well-founded on reality, and that the fear can do more harm than the reality. We act as though our highest priority is to prevent our children from growing up into murderous thugs—but modern kids are far more likely to grow up too passive, too distrustful of themselves, too easily manipulated.

We send the message to our children in a hundred ways that their craving for imaginary gun battles and symbolic killings is wrong, or at least dangerous. Even when we don't call for censorship or forbid [the video game] "Mortal Kombat," we moan to other parents within our kids' earshot about the "awful violence" in the entertainment they love. We tell our kids that it isn't nice to play-fight, or we steer them from some monstrous action figure to a pro-social doll. Even in the most progressive households, where we make such a point of letting children feel what they feel, we rush to substitute an enlightened discussion for the raw material of rageful fantasy. In the process, we risk confusing them about their natural aggression in the same way the Victorians confused their children about their sexuality. When we try to protect our children from their own feelings and fantasies, we shelter them not against violence but against power and selfhood.

> "In pro wrestling . . . humiliation, control,
> and verbal aggression . . . is the way that
> 'real men' prevail."

Professional Wrestling
Promotes Violent Behavior

Jackson Katz and Sut Jhally

In the following viewpoint Jackson Katz and Sut Jhally argue
that the depictions of violent masculinity on televised professional wrestling shows are a step backward in the evolution of
male and female roles. According to Katz and Jhally, professional wrestling culture promotes the idea that real men are
violent and aggressive while real women are sex objects. The
authors also claim that professional wrestling inspires increased bullying and disrespect for women. Katz is a writer,
activist, and public speaker; Jhally is the author (with Justin
Lewis) of *Enlightened Racism: The Cosby Show, Audiences, and
the Myth of the American Dream.*

As you read, consider the following questions:

1. What observations do the authors make about
   professional wrestling's association with homosexuality?
2. How does pro wrestling inspire bullying behavior,
   according to Katz and Jhally?
3. According to the authors, how does pro wrestling depict
   sexuality?

Jackson Katz and Sut Jhally, "Manhood on the Mat," *Boston Globe*, February 13,
2000. Copyright © 2000 by Jackson Katz and Sut Jhally. Reproduced by
permission.

As professional wrestling explodes in popularity, cultural analysts are struggling to catch up to its significance for society. The traditional ways of seeing it—for example, as a morality play of good vs. evil—have been transcended, as wrestling has morphed into perhaps the ultimate expression of the entertainment industry's new, multiplexed model for success.

Vince McMahon, head of the World Wrestling Federation,[1] describes it as "contemporary sports entertainment which treats 'professional wrestling' as an action/adventure soap opera. With the sexuality of '90210,' the subject matter of 'NYPD Blue,' the athleticism of the Olympics, combined with reality-based story lines, the WWF presents a hybrid of almost all forms of entertainment and sports combined in one show." Add to that the fertile brew of traditional advertising, product merchandising, and frequent pay-per-view special events and the result is revenue in the tens of millions of dollars, not to mention a forceful new strain of sports entertainment.

But understanding pro wrestling's immense popularity, especially with (white) men and boys, requires viewing it in the broader context of shifting gender relations.

New Definitions of Masculinity

The accomplishments of social movements such as feminism, as well as the shift to a postindustrial, high-tech era of automated production and e-commerce, have challenged the culture to construct new definitions of masculinity. In the new social, cultural, and employment context, there is less emphasis on characteristics such as strength and physicality that, in an earlier age, not only clearly defined men and women in very different ways, but made masculinity dominant.

In threatened response, many men have retreated into the safe and cartoonish masculinity of a more primal gender order, a world typified by the wildly popular program "WWF Smackdown!" where size, strength, and brutality are rewarded. In wrestling's contemporary incarnation, it's not

1. The World Wrestling Federation (WWF) has been renamed World Wrestling Entertainment (WWE).

who wins and loses that matters, but how the game is played. And the way the game is played in the WWF and its companion league, World Championship Wrestling, or WCW, reinforces the prime directive—might makes right, with extreme violence defining how power is exercised.

In the past, discussions about wrestling's effects on "real world" violence have typically centered on the behavioral effects of exposure to it. Does it cause imitative violence? But that misses the point. For the question is not, "Are children imitating the violence they see?" but "Are children learning that taunting, ridiculing, and bullying define masculinity?"

We know from decades of research that depictions of violence in the entertainment media create a cultural climate in which such behavior is accepted as a normal, even appropriate, response to various problems.

Real Men

We can see this process of normalization clearly in pro wrestling, where intimidation, humiliation, control, and verbal aggression (toward men as well as women) is the way that "real men" prevail. Manhood is equated explicitly with the ability to settle scores, defend one's honor, and win respect and compliance through force of conquest.

Already, this definition of manhood is at the root of much interpersonal violence in our society. For example, abusive men use force (or the threat of it) in an attempt to exercise power and control in their relationships with women. While there is no causal relationship between pro wrestling and male violence, it is clear that the wrestling subculture contributes to a larger cultural environment that teaches boys and men that manhood is about achieving power and control.

Real (or simulated) physical violence actually comprises a small percentage of the length of a pro wrestling telecast. Most of the time is devoted to setting up the narratives, and to verbal confrontation and bullying. In wrestling video games, each combatant not only has signature moves, but also verbal taunts that can be directed against either an opponent or the crowd. The object of the game is to see who can be the most effective bully.

It is a lesson that resonates all too clearly in our schools: A recent survey of 6,000 children in grades 4 to 6 found that about 1 in 10 said they were bullied one or more times a week, and 1 in 5 admitted to being bullies themselves. And we know from the 1990s' series of school shootings that, all too often, guns become the great equalizer for boys who have been bullied, ridiculed, and verbally taunted.

Imitating Pro Wrestlers

Unfortunately, many adolescent boys are imitating [the behaviors they see in professional wrestling matches]. Nationwide, teens are staging wrestling matches in their back yards, complete with the pile drivers and sexual innuendo they see on television. There are backyard wrestling groups in 30 states.

Ted Rueter, *USA Today*, March 30, 2000.

The hyper-masculine wrestling subculture is also deeply infused with homophobic anxiety. Macho posturing and insults ("wimps," and other worse epithets) can barely mask the fear of feminization that is always present in the homoerotic entanglement of male bodies. (The most popular of the trademark taunts by the wrestler X-Pac involves a thrusting of the crotch, accompanied by a sexual vulgarity, and his signature move of humiliation is to back his opponent into a corner and "ride" his face.)

Degrading to Women

As the enactment of gender has moved to center stage in wrestling narratives, so have women become much more central to the plot lines. In the days of Hulk Hogan and the Macho Man, women were essentially restricted to a couple of sexualized figures. But now, there are many stereotypically hyper-sexualized female characters, especially in the WWF.

More frequently male wrestlers have "girlfriends" who accompany them to the ring. And every week, in one of the most overtly racist and sexist characterizations on contemporary television, the Godfather, an over-the-top stereotype of a hustling pimp (and one of the few important black figures in the WWF) leads out his "ho train" of scantily-clad white women to the leering and jeering crowds.

As female sexuality is increasingly used in the scripts, the line between the bimbo/prostitute sidekick and the female wrestlers is eroding. A recent WWF women's champion is Miss Kitty, a former hyper-sexualized sidekick, who during one pay-per-view event removed her top. And the big contests for female wrestlers often involve mud or chocolate baths, or the "evening dress" contest (where you lose by having your dress ripped from your body).

The few exceptions, such as Chyna, a wrestler in her own right, (who, with The Rock, graced . . . *Newsweek* magazine cover) emerge from another place in heterosexual male fantasy, the Amazon warrior—tall, muscular, lithe, and buxom.

While ambiguity about proper gender assignments may be the contemporary norm, in the mock-violent world of professional wrestling, masculinity and femininity are clearly defined. And while pro wrestling shares many of the values sometimes associated with elements of the political far right (among them patriarchy, opposition to homosexuality, and respect for hierarchy), many conservatives have condemned its vulgarity and sexuality.

This criticism (much of it egged on by master promoters like McMahon) fuels the erroneous belief of some youngsters that somehow the WWF and WCW are alternative and rebellious. However, one of the great insights of cultural studies is that adherence to a conservative and repressive gender order can appear powerful and liberating—or rebellious—even as it assigns greater suffering to those deemed less powerful in the social order.

Some people will argue that analyzing the social impact of wrestling is a useless exercise because, after all, it's only play acting, right? But to those who still believe that there is no connection between popular culture and broader social and political issues, that an analysis of wrestling has nothing to teach us about where our culture is heading, we have two words of caution: Jesse Ventura [former wrestler and later governor of Minnesota].

"What other form of entertainment offers such a pure and timeless theme, complete with sing-along catchphrases and comic book personas?"

Professional Wrestling Is Harmless Drama

Ray Deonandan

Ray Deonandan argues in the following viewpoint that professional wrestling offers fans harmless high drama. He contends that the sport does not promote violence because viewers know the contests are scripted. Moreover, unlike real athletes who hurt one another in anger, professional wrestlers work hard to avoid harming each other. Deonandan is an epidemiologist and author of many books and articles.

As you read, consider the following questions:

1. According to Deonandan, what do wrestling's critics not understand about it?
2. How is pro wrestling interactive, according to the author?
3. According to the author, why is pro wrestling not similar to the battles of ancient gladiators?

Ray Deonandan, "Why I Love Professional Wrestling," www.deonandan.com, December 17, 2001. Copyright © 2001 by Raywat Deonandan. Reproduced by permission.

Sometimes I think I'd be more comfortable admitting to a criminal conviction or a sexual deviancy. Certainly, to some minds, my dirty little secret could be put in the same category. It's a private shame that I try to avow early in any relationship, bringing it to the forefront to be discussed and laughed about, the theory being that ad hoc truthfulness vitiates the foul deed. Yet despite my outward comfort—nay pride—in this particular deviant taste, I must confess to a daily struggle to explain to the unbelievers why, oh why, I so love the "sport" of professional wrestling.

The look of horror on the faces of those to whom I have offered this confession is a universal. Since wrestling's recent explosion into the true mainstream, courtesy mostly of The Rock's bellicose pop culture appeal, that look has become hidden behind stolid faces of straining nonjudgmentalism. But it lingers still, a silent scream of disgust and pity, its unspoken (and sometimes loudly spoken) plea one of tiresome redundance to my sighing ear: "How can someone so educated and intelligent watch such crap?"

Drama, Not Sport

Usually, I then launch into my practiced lecture about the ancient and pure nature of wrestling, its timbre resonating with that of Greek theatre, its core morality play identical to history's finest examples of good drama. While few ever buy the argument, they are usually sufficiently impressed by my liberal use of big words to gather that I've at least given the issue some thought—more so, dare I say it, than do people who watch supposedly "high brow" television, like *cough hack* Bill Maher's *Politically Incorrect* or *Law & Order*, which are as equally exploitative but rarely vilified.

You see, I do not enjoy watching real sports. I don't believe in glorifying the questionable accomplishments of thin-brained 20-year-olds whose incomes criminally exceed the economies of many small nations. I particularly question the permissability of fighting in ice hockey, scenarios in which genuinely angry grown men try to physically harm one another. At least in wrestling, the violence is fake and the wrestlers strenuously work to avoid injuring one another.

Detractors invariably point out that the fans don't know

that it's fake, and so wrestling shows simply stoke a public bloodthirst. To such critics, I can only sigh, their ignorance being a blight upon all good sense. I don't think I'll be crushing any dreams when I say here, in print, that everyone knows that wrestling outcomes are predetermined, and that everyone knows that most of the brutality is illusory. Yes, even many of the children. To my thinking, such detractors expose their own poor understanding and poor faith in the thrum of modern society.

The Well-Educated Wrestling Fan

Today's professional wrestling fans aren't your father's wrestling fans. We are well-educated, well-adjusted, reside above the Mason-Dixon Line—and understand we aren't watching an actual sporting event. Some of us even cover those so-called real sports for a living.

Ron Buck, ESPN.com, April 2, 1999.

Moreover, the enjoyableness of professional wrestling is not related to that of a genuine gladiatorial contest. On the whole, fans do not seek brutality as the outcome. Instead, we simply seek a well told story set in a weird world of supermen and thin egos. Therein lies the secret power of this genre. We don't watch Monday Night Raw looking for a kind of realistic Ali-Foreman contest. No, we watch it hoping for a Rocky–Apollo Creed finale: a staged movie payoff to a well crafted preceding drama.

Good Versus Evil

In the wrestling world, Evil invariably faces off against Good, with Good always coming out on top. In the interim, Evil only wins when Evil cheats, but will always get its just deserts in the end. What other form of entertainment offers such a pure and timeless theme, complete with sing-along catchphrases and comic book personas? The stories told in the modern era are wonders to behold. Brother against brother, marital betrayal, love, tragedy, returns from the dead, behind-the-scenes politicking, teams torn asunder by misunderstanding or greed—all these stories eventually lead to a physical contest inside the fabled "squared circle", and all must be told simultaneously to a live audience of tens of thousands and to a television audience of millions. When Stone Cold Steve Austin drinks a beer at the end of his match, his practiced flourishes must be as well seen by those in the back row of the arena as by those watching close-up on the TV screen, testament both to Austin's unique acting ability and to the need to keep every single audience member engaged. Unlike other TV offerings, wrestling is tweaked day to day to respond to audience reaction. Storylines are radically rewritten or abandoned in mid-stride if fans respond unfavourably. No other entertainment genre offers such interactivity and complexity of performance.

Admittedly, there are elements to this entertainment genre which are disturbing, its occasional sexism and racism being obvious examples. At present, the WWF [World Wrestling Federation] in particular suffers not from excessive offensiveness, but simply from lackadaisical writing. I have thus questioned if the present lacklustre product has stifled my innate love for the "sport." I have searched for an image or moment which could rekindle the flame of my fandom. I found it in a recent match between The Rock and Chris Jericho.

Jericho, a well-liked underdog, had just beaten ultimate fan-favourite The Rock for the WCW [World Championship Wrestling] Championship, but had resorted to an illegal chair-shot to do so. In the post-match showdown, Jericho clutched his uncleanly won belt with ambiguous joy as The Rock approached him with the steel chair cocked to deliver a retributive blow. No words were spoken. Instead of delivering the expected blow, however, The Rock just handed Jericho the chair and marched out of the ring, leaving the new champion to his tainted celebration. It was the look on Jericho's face that sold the moment to me. Without speaking a word or raising a fist, he communicated that he had criminally bloodied his hands to attain his goal, commencing on a hubris-strewn path of tragedy which would eventually lead to his downfall. His shame was palpable, but subtle. It was a Macbeth moment that calls to the heart of good drama, and which encourages me to declare yet again that I am a proud fan of professional wrestling.

> *"Yet cultural manifestations of some of the nastier aspects of society are far easier to put forward than the realities of life that might have created [them]."*

Violent Rap Lyrics Are Not a Significant Contributor to Violent Behavior

Pat Stack

In the following viewpoint Pat Stack contends that many people mistakenly blame gun violence on violent rap lyrics because it is easier to do so than to address the underlying societal problems such as poverty that actually contribute to violent crime. Stack grants that some rap lyrics are objectionable, but he insists that they do not lead to violence. Throughout history, he asserts, some maladjusted people have been inspired by violent lyrics to commit crimes, but he points out that banning such lyrics is unlikely to reduce violence in any significant way. Pat Stack is a columnist for *Socialist Review*.

As you read, consider the following questions:

1. What factors were implicated in the Columbine High School massacre, according to Stack?
2. According to Stack, what are some examples of violent entertainment directly linked to violent acts?
3. What criticisms of rap lyrics does the author make?

Pat Stack, "Talking Rap," *Socialist Review*, February 2003. Copyright © 2003 by *Socialist Review*. Reproduced by permission.

I remember just after the Columbine massacre[1] hearing some right wing American shock-jock being interviewed as to why the massacre had happened. The music of Marilyn Manson, video nasties, and lack of parental control were all cited. When the interviewer asked whether gun control might not help, the shock-jock dismissed this as so much liberal hooey.

Culture and Society

Now it may seem obvious that CDs or indeed videos are not much use as weapons of any kind of destruction, and that a gun is, by any standards, a potentially lethal weapon. But it didn't even occur to this jerk that he sounded absurd. Yet cultural manifestations of some of the nastier aspects of society are far easier to put forward than the realities of life that might have created these nastier aspects.

The rather glib . . . rallying cry of "Tough on crime, tough on the causes of crime" becomes even glibber when a government minister reveals that the "causes of crime" are actually a motley group of rappers. He later added violent play-station games. That, though, appears to be what "culture" (God help us) secretary Kim Howells believes. In the aftermath of the Birmingham shootings [where four teenage girls were killed in January 2003] we need apparently look no further than rap music in general and the "macho idiot rappers" of So Solid Crew in particular, and video games, to explain "gun culture", "black on black crime", and general "lawlessness" and "hooliganism".

This black on black crime stuff fascinates me. I live in an area of London where there have been a number of violent drug-related deaths over the past few months [in 2003], and the ethnic mix of killers and killed has been great. Nobody in the area is going on about Greek on Italian crime or second generation Irish on English crime.

An Easy Target

How handy, though, that music and video are there so that we don't need any of that liberal guff about poverty, lack of

1. On April 20, 1999, two students at a Colorado high school went on a shooting spree, killing twelve students, a teacher, and themselves.

resources, alienation, or any of those other things that [British prime minister Tony] Blair has failed to deal with to explain violent crime. Like the mad rantings of the shock-jock, one is forced to stand back from this and wonder at the inanity of it all.

Reflecting Reality

Hip-hop has always drawn much of its creative energy from the underworld. Take the names of the record labels—Death Row, Murder Inc., Bad Boy—or the style: wearing trousers that fall from the waist comes from prison, where inmates are not allowed to wear belts. If American legislators were serious about stopping the violence associated with rap music, they might start with the gun laws and penal system that create the reality reflected in the lyrics.

Gary Younge, *Guardian*, January 10, 2003.

Indeed how strange that this pillar of the New Labour intelligentsia needs to have a member of So Solid Crew explain to him that their music merely reflected "real life issues and what's going on on the streets . . . you can't blame So Solid for all the gun violence out there". So banal is this truism, that you would hardly think it worth stating. Yet clearly it has passed Howells by.

Howells is a strange man. A student radical influenced by Trotskyism [a type of socialism] in 1968, he studied at Hornsey College of Art, renowned for its student militancy and avant-garde attitude to art. Almost uniquely among his generation, he moved from the fringes of Trotskyism to the staid grey world of the Communist Party of Great Britain. From there he trod a more common path to union officialdom, and finally to his latest incarnation, that of Blairite cultural fuddy duddy.

Violent Lyrics Are Not New

It is crucial that the left doesn't fall for his line. True, some rap lyrics are unpleasant, nihilistic, homophobic, and/or misogynist, and some of the artists are far from pleasant people. Yet rap also finds an echo in the realities of modern urban life, and reflects anger and alienation, and to cast haughty judgement on it is little better than my parents telling me that the Rolling Stones were nasty and that you "couldn't hear the words".

Ah, it's said, but their violent lyrics are causing all the violence. Now it would be foolish of me to say that there isn't some vulnerable messed up soul out there who, having listened to the lyrics of some song, decided to do something violent. But I have no idea where this gets us. After all, the guy who tried to assassinate [President] Ronnie Reagan claimed that his love for Jodie Foster, after having seen her in the classic *Taxi Driver*, was the cause for his act of violence. Should we conclude that the film should be banned (or, come to think of it, shown daily in all public places)?

An entire terrorist movement in the United States in the late 1960s, the Weathermen, took their name from a line in a Bob Dylan song. When Charles Manson and his crew murdered Sharon Tate and others they scrawled the words "Piggies" all over the wall. It was a direct lift from a Beatles song. Indeed the Beatles recorded a song which went "Happiness is a warm gun, bang bang shoot shoot". No doubt it became an anthem for "white on white crime" at the time.

I also think I have discovered the origin of [the terrorist group] Al Qaida. A singer in the 1960s released a song called "I'm Gonna Get Me a Gun". It included the lines,

And all those people who put me down
You better get ready to run
Cuz I'm gonna get me a gun.

His name was Cat Stevens. He later changed it to Yusuf Islam on converting to Islam. Now I reckon that in his pre-radical days when he lived in London [terrorist] Osama Bin Laden would, on his way to watch Arsenal on a Saturday afternoon, be listening to his co-religionist's classic on a Walkman, and as a result turned to the gun and violent means to reach his political ends.

Ah, to live in the simple world of Kim Howells—lock up Martin Scorsese, Bob Dylan, the Beatles, Cat Stevens, Eminem and So Solid Crew and you've done away with all the evil in the world. No drug-related crime, no urban terror, no mad assassins, no 11 September, and all at little or no cost.

Culture minister? Why the man should be home secretary [the British government official responsible for domestic safety and justice]. Watch out [Home Secretary David] Blunkett! He's comin' to get ya.

"Words do have meanings, meanings suggest thoughts, and thoughts lead to action."

Violent Rap Lyrics Can Encourage Violent Behavior

Brent Morrison

Brent Morrison argues in the following viewpoint that violent lyrics can lead to aggressive behavior. Morrison grants that well-adjusted listeners would probably not be adversely affected by violent rap lyrics. However, he maintains that words can inevitably lead to actions, thus rap lyrics could promote violence in some listeners. Brent Morrison is a columnist whose writings focus on the impact of the choices people face every day.

As you read, consider the following questions:

1. According to Morrison, what do young people report liking about rap music?
2. What criticism does the author have of recent research implicating rap lyrics in violent behavior?
3. What analogue does the author provide to the old saying, "We are what we eat"?

Brent Morrison, "Mean Music: Violent Lyrics and Aggression," http://brentmorrison.com, May 12, 2003. Copyright © 2003 by Brent Morrison. Reproduced by permission.

It's not exactly stated, but a report issued by the American Psychological Association this month [May 2003] seems to conclude that words mean things.

I like to think so when I write anyway, though the study deals specifically with violent lyrics in songs. It's a subject worthy of consideration; the content of any CD that doesn't have a picture of Elmo on it is suspect these days.

The average adolescent will argue that the words don't matter. They just like the beat, the rhythm, the guitar solos, the picture on the cover, the crinkle of the shrink-wrap, that new plastic smell, anything but the actual message. It's tempting to believe them given how many vocals are recorded in an angry mumble only eardrums under the age of 25 can understand, and that when you do catch a fragment you'll probably wish you hadn't.

Aggressive Thoughts

In experiments on over 500 college students, who often work cheaper than guinea pigs and have less complicated musical tastes, subjects were found to experience an increase in aggressive thoughts after listening to songs with violent lyrics. Those subjected to the mean music were more apt to connect hostile meanings to words deemed to be violence neutral by the researchers.

The words used in the study as "clearly aggressive" were blood, butcher, choke, fight, gun, hatchet, hurt, kill, knife, and wound. I understand that not everyone sees things the same way, but I worry about people who read hostility into inanimate objects like guns, hatchets, and knives. And to me, a butcher is the friendly old guy who had the shop at the end of the block when I was a kid, blood is the essence of life, and choked up is how I feel when I see a butterfly at sunrise.

OK I got carried away, but you see the problem. The so-called "ambiguous" words are just as debatable: alley, animal, bottle, drugs, movie, night, police, red, rock, and stick. "Police" is probably as good a one-word Rorschach test any but everyone knows that sticks and stones can break your bones. If you don't think "movie" is inherently violent you probably haven't wandered into a theater lately.

Still, let's assume the choice of aggressive and neutral words was appropriate. The study found that the style of music had nothing to do with increased hostility. Thus "Mary Had a Little Lamb" performed by the hard rock band Korn would not increase aggression even though it wouldn't be confused for a lullaby. Barry Manilow crooning rap lyrics might start a riot.

Glamorizing Violence

Producing, promoting, and peddling violent music to children is not merely scandalous, it is dangerous. Marketing messages of hate and violence to children sends the signal that violence is widespread and normal, that it is acceptable to abuse women, and that there is glamour in lawlessness. Whatever we glamorize, we encourage; a society that glorifies violence—in music or elsewhere—will surely grow more violent.

Sam Brownback, *Policy Review*, November/December 1998.

Aggression levels also went up after listening to humorous violent songs, which seemed like an oxymoron until I recalled the homicidal "Maxwell's Silver Hammer" by that noted death-rock ensemble, the Beatles. And what about Tom Jones? Good heavens, if he were a rap star every album he ever released would have a parental advisory warning.

Not that teens are flocking to buy the latest Tom Jones CDs. They probably don't like the beat. In any event if Jones' fifty-something female fans have ever torn up a Las Vegas nightclub I haven't heard of it.

Words Matter

Despite my quibbles with some of its points, the study's basic conclusion is right on the mark. Words do have meanings, meanings suggest thoughts, and thoughts lead to action. Most reasonably well-adjusted people will suffer no lasting harm from occasional exposure to violent content, but it doesn't take a study to figure out that the constant pounding of nasty messages from music, television, movies, video games, and other amusements have a cumulative impact.

It is said that we are what we eat; I'd argue that we become what we think. If so, perhaps we should pay as much attention to our entertainment diets as our waistlines.

Periodical Bibliography

The following articles have been selected to supplement the diverse views presented in this chapter.

Debashis Aikat	"Streaming Violent Genres Online: Visual Images in Music Videos on BET.com, Country.com, MTV.com, VH1.com," *Popular Music and Society*, June 2004.
Craig Anderson, Nicholas Carnagey, and Janie Eubanks	"Exposure to Violent Media: The Effects of Songs with Violent Lyrics on Aggressive Thoughts and Feelings," *Journal of Personality and Social Psychology*, 2003.
Craig Anderson and Brad J. Bushman	"The Effects of Media Violence on Society," *Science Magazine*, March 2002.
Lillian R. BeVier	"Controlling Communications That Teach or Demonstrate Violence: 'The Movie Made Them Do It,'" *Journal of Law, Medicine, and Ethics*, Spring 2004.
Audrey M. Buchanan et al.	"What Goes in Must Come Out: Children's Media Violence Consumption at Home and Aggressive Behaviors at School," *Journal of Applied Developmental Psychology*, 2002.
Larry Elder	"Desensitivity Training," June 11, 1999. www.frontpagemag.com.
Kevin Fagan	"Video Games: Glorifying Gore, Mayhem for Minors," *San Francisco Chronicle*, July 7, 2002.
Jonah Goldberg	"Violent Fantasy: It's Not the Hollywood Gore That's the Problem," *National Review*, October 23, 2000.
Daphne Lavers	"The Verdict on Media Violence," *Insight on the News*, May 13, 2002.
Monique A. Levermore	"Violent Media and Videogames, and Their Role in Creating Violent Youth," *Forensic Examiner*, Fall 2004.
Paul Neumarkt	"The Age of Violence," *Journal of Evolutionary Psychology*, March 2004.
Jeffrey Overstreet	"Do Movies Kill People?" *Christianity Today*, August 16, 2001.
Todd Shields	"FCC Likely to Investigate Violence in the Media," *Media Week*, March 29, 2004.
Susan Villani	"Impact of Media on Children and Adolescents: A Ten-Year Review of the Research," *Journal of the American Academy of Child and Adolescent Psychiatry*, April 2001.

CHAPTER 4

What Values Does Popular Culture Promote?

Chapter Preface

A contentious debate rages over the powerful influence the media wields in shaping society's values. Many conservatives perceive popular culture as a threat to traditional religious and sexual beliefs and practices. Numerous liberals applaud the expansion of freedom of expression and believe popular culture is advancing knowledge and diversity. The debate over popular culture's influence has its roots in social changes that occurred after World War II.

During the first half of the twentieth century, Americans assumed that popular culture's central role was to reinforce the values promoted by traditional institutions—churches and synagogues, public schools, and government. For example, during World War II, Hollywood produced film after film urging patriotic sacrifice and support for the American war effort. Nudity and graphic displays of affection in movies were prohibited, in keeping with traditional moral values. During the second half of the twentieth century, however, the role of popular culture began to change. Movies, television programs, musical recordings, and literature largely abdicated their former role as guardians of traditional values and instead became avenues for personal expression and the examination of existing norms.

This change in popular culture coincided with a decline in the influence of the institution that had long been the main arbiter of moral values—mainstream organized religion. Between 1965 and 1990, for example, mainstream Protestant churches lost between a fifth and a third of their membership. As a result of this decline, organized religion's ability to unify the country began to erode. In consequence, values became more diverse, and the liberal, secular left began to dominate pop culture. Soon popular culture began to abandon its self-imposed censorship. Beginning in the late 1960s and early 1970s, graphic depictions of sexuality and violence in movies greatly increased in number. Lyrics in rock music became more suggestive, and pornography began to earn a degree of respectability. Partially in response to these changes in popular culture, which many perceived as an assault on traditional moral values, a religious backlash of sorts occurred.

Membership increased in the smaller Southern Baptist and Catholic denominations, which tend to be more conservative. As popular culture became more liberal, segments of the population became more conservative. The result has been a more culturally polarized country.

As events in the twentieth century illustrate, popular culture can have an enormous impact on society. The viewpoints in the following chapter explore the values that popular culture continues to shape.

"Hollywood hates authentic Christians because Christianity is diametrically opposed to its worldview."

The Movie Industry Fosters Anti-Religious Attitudes

Don Feder

In the following viewpoint Don Feder maintains that Hollywood is hostile to religion in general and Christianity in particular because Hollywood's values are inconsistent with Christianity's. The author lists a series of recent films that have mocked or vilified Christians and Christianity, and he claims that by attacking Christians, Hollywood is advancing its own secular, leftist agenda. Don Feder, a former *Boston Herald* writer, is a political and communications consultant.

As you read, consider the following questions:

1. According to Feder, what stereotypes of Christians routinely appear in Hollywood movies?
2. Why is Hollywood afraid of Christians, according to the author?
3. According to Feder, when did Hollywood become hostile to Christianity?

Don Feder, "Why Hollywood Hates Christianity," www.FrontPageMag.com, May 31, 2004. Copyright © 2004 by the Center for the Study of Popular Culture. Reproduced by permission.

W hat do you get when you cross the village atheist with the village idiot? *Saved*—the alleged comedy polluting theaters nationwide this weekend [May 2004].

Recall the wailing and hand-wringing that accompanied the release of Mel Gibson's *The Passion of the Christ*, in February. Given the hysterical reaction to Gibson's opus, you'd think Hollywood had suddenly become an adjunct of "The 700 Club" [Pat Robertson's daily evangelical news broadcast]. But *The Passion* was an aberration that never would have been made without the influence of its famous producer/director.

Saved is far more typical of the way the movie industry does religion these days. The teen sex comedy is politically correct, tedious, nasty and loaded with anti-Christian stereotypes.

The heroine, Mary, attends a Christian academy—American Eagle Christian High School—a combination of the Valley Girls' school in "Clueless" and a parody of a revival meeting.

Mary learns her boyfriend has homosexual tendencies. Jesus comes to her in a vision—Jesus and Mary, get it?—and commands the good girl to do everything in her power to save the lad. She ends up pregnant and ostracized by the school's Bible-belt Barbie in-crowd.

Mary joins the academy's misfits, including a Jewish girl who claims she's an ex-stripper—in modern movies, Jews are okay, as long as they're safely secular—a skateboarder, and a wheelchair-bound cynic, played by a grownup Macauley Culkin, who would have been better off at home, alone.

Naturally, the outcasts are all swell kids, while the Christian students are portrayed as Nazi airheads.

Why Hollywood Hates Christians

What's more interesting than this latest cinematic assault on Christianity, is the mind-set behind it: Not how, but *why* Hollywood hates the followers of Jesus.

Since at least the 1970s, Hollywood's treatment of Christians has been only slightly more benevolent than [the Islamic terrorist group] al-Qaeda's attitude toward Jews.

Gone are the kindly Barry Fitzgerald priest, the wise rabbi and the steadfast minister. In their place is a rogue's gallery of lusting priests, sadistic nuns, perverted pastors and con-men TV evangelists—not to mention ordinary Christians (Catholic or evangelical) who are depicted as superstitious nitwits, malevolent hypocrites, or both.

Saved joins the Hollywood hit parade of blasphemy and slander, including:

- *The Last Temptation of Christ* (1988)—wherein Jesus is given a fantasy sex life.
- *Priest* (1994)—a good, homosexual priest battles "re-pression" in his Church and heterosexual incest.
- *Dogma* (1999)—another reputed comedy, wherein an abortion clinic worker (the perfect heroine, from Hol-lywood's perspective) and the great-grand-niece of Jesus (?) save the world from destruction by fallen angels try-ing to enter a church to reenter Heaven. Don't ask. When it comes to an opportunity to bash Christians, no plot is too ridiculous.
- *The Magdalene Sisters* (2003)—set in a convent school run by nuns who could pass as concentration-camp guards.
- *The Order* (2003)—teen heartthrob Heath Ledger bat-tles yet another secret order within the Roman Catholic Church bent on no-good.
- *Stigmata* (1999)—the entire Roman Catholic Church is shown to be hiding the "real" Gospel, and a priest tries to *murder* its last true disciple.
- *The Saint* (1997)—frequently, anti-Christian characteri-zations bear little or no relation to a movie's plot. They are gratuitous, but damaging nonetheless. This movie opens in a Far Eastern orphanage run by a brutal priest who beats and starves the children and is responsible for the death of one of his charges.

Along the same lines, but somewhat more restrained, there's the paddle-wielding priest in *The Basketball Diaries* (1995) and the brother who thinks he's Mike Tyson in *Heaven Help Us* (1985).

Hollywood's Anti-Christian Crusade

The above only skims the surface of Hollywood's anti-Christian crusade. As they do in so many areas, movies shape popular attitudes and perceptions here as well. According to the Barna Group, the percentage of Americans who only attend religious services for holidays or on special occasions, increased from 21 percent in 1991 to 34 percent today.

When it comes to different denominations, Hollywood isn't an equal-opportunity offender. Here's a short lists of religious groups it wouldn't dream of baiting: Unitarians, Presbyterians, members of any liberal, Protestant denomination, Cafeteria Catholics, Reform Jews, Buddhists, Wiccans and Moslems. (Producers and directors may be anti-religion, but they aren't suicidal.)

The Persecution of Mel Gibson

While some critics want to focus on alleged anti-Semitism in the film, how about raising the subject of anti-Christian bigotry? The elites who have lambasted [Mel] Gibson [for producing the film *The Passion of the Christ*] said nothing about Martin Scorsese's blasphemous and historically inaccurate film, *The Last Temptation of Christ*. Now that Gibson has made a film mostly in line with what the Bible says, he is treated as an infidel and bigot by many of his peers.

Cal Thomas, Townhall.com, February 23, 2004.

Why are traditional Catholics, evangelicals and—to a lesser extent—Orthodox Jews, considered fair game?

Because the Hollywood Left (in other words, 98 percent of the self-styled artistic community) views them as the enemy—more even than the military (which occasionally come off well in action films) and corporate executives, and about on par with the CIA, Southern sheriffs, Republicans and companies bulldozing the Brazilian rainforest.

Hollywood hates authentic Christians because Christianity is diametrically opposed to its worldview—a dogma reflected in the very deep thoughts of Michael Moore, Tim Robbins and Barbra (color me stupid) Streisand. It's based on the following tenets:

1. *Sexual Liberation*—the glorification of pre-marital sex (including adolescent experimentation), adultery, homosexuality, abortion and the sexualization of children. This may be contrasted with the Judeo-Christian ethic of sexual restraint/responsibility, and the sanctification of sex

within marriage (raising the carnal to a spiritual plane).

2. *A Live-for-the-Moment Ethos*—the here-and-now is all there is, or as the beer commercial used to put it, "You only go around once; so grab all the gusto you can." This is opposed to the Christian emphasis on life eternal. Christians and religious Jews live not for the moment but for eternity. Hollywood's seize-the-moment ethic must ultimately lead to a total rejection of the Ten Commandments and all biblical morality.

3. *The Cult of Self*—or to put it in the lingo of pop psychology: "self-actualization," really self-gratification. From this perspective, putting anything ahead of your own happiness is dumb, if not psychotic. Christianity and Judaism both teach that your life isn't your own. It belongs to the One who gave you life.

4. *Gender Sameness*—the bizarre and amply refuted doctrine that men and women are psychologically identical, that gender roles are socially imposed, instead of reality-based. This dogma lies at the heart of liberalism's push to radically remake the family. The worse invective the Left can hurl at the family (from its perspective) is "patriarchal" and "male-dominated."

5. *Militant Secularism*—the belief that religious expression should be confined to a white clapboard building, and that traditional faith should play no role in shaping our laws and institutions. Thus, someone who speaks of rights being "endowed by their Creator" (like the Founding Fathers) or saying that America is a nation "under God" (like Abraham Lincoln) becomes an enemy of democracy.

Fear of Christianity

What really enrages the Hollywood Left is the realization that, more than any other group in our society, evangelical Christians—who now constitute the nation's largest identifiable voting bloc—stand in the way of its political agenda: abortion on demand, a contraceptive culture, erotic indoctrination masquerading as sex education, universal day care (the literal Nanny State), the complete societal blessing of gay marriage and hate-crimes legislation that criminalizes religious speech. By attacking Christians, Hollywood is advancing its agenda.

Actually, it is to the credit of Christians that Hollywood considers them the enemy. Similarly, Jews can take pride in the fact that, in the 20th century, both communists and Nazis hated them, as do Islamacists today.

Over the past 40 years, Hollywood has been primarily responsible for the rapid degeneration of our culture. Modern cinema is filled with violence, sadism, sex at its most animalistic, crudeness, nihilism and despair. If Hollywood wants to treat Christianity as the antithesis of all it holds dear, Christians should feel complimented.

"*Any producer can get a hearing from Hollywood right now if they say, 'I have a movie for the audience who loved* The Passion [of the Christ].'"

The Movie Industry Has Begun to Foster Respect for Religion

Barbara Nicolosi

According to Barbara Nicolosi in the following viewpoint, there is a new hunger for spirituality in Hollywood. In recent years there has been an increase in religious and spiritual content in both movies and television, Nicolosi states. Young filmmakers are rejecting violent and sexual themes and choosing instead to make movies that explore life's ultimate meaning, she contends. Nicolosi believes that Christians should take this opportunity to expand their creative influence on Hollywood. Barbara Nicolosi is the founder of Act One, a Christian screenwriters group in Hollywood.

As you read, consider the following questions:

1. According to Nicolosi, what evidence is there that Hollywood is undergoing a spiritual awakening?
2. In the wake of the success of *The Passion of the Christ*, what should Christian filmmakers do to improve the morality of movies, according to the author?
3. According to Nicolosi, how has *The Passion of the Christ* impacted society?

Barbara Nicolosi, "Reasons for Hope from Hollywood," www.catholic.org, May 28, 2004. Copyright © 2004 by Catholic Online. Reproduced by permission of the publisher and author.

I do not often have the opportunity to speak to audiences that bring together both sides of my personal reality as both a Catholic and a filmmaker. Sadly, there have been far too few of this kind of discussions in the Catholic Church. For many reasons, including a kind of intellectual elitism, Catholic scholars have been slow to appreciate the power of cinema as both an art form and as a means of evangelization.

I will talk today [May 13, 2004] about a few recent movements in the secular entertainment industry, and how these might be positive for the Church. I want to demonstrate why the Church should embrace this art form as a powerful gift of God, using as an example "The Passion of the Christ." Then, I will suggest some areas in which the Church can help mainstream cinema.

A Search for Meaning

In January 2003, I got a call from a woman who was recently profiled in the Writers Guild of America magazine as one of the top 10 women in television. As the executive producer and head writer on a hit TV show, this woman belongs to an elite club of people on the whole planet. Her prime-time CBS show gets a weekly audience in the States of around 20 million people, and globally probably twice that many more.

The gist of her call to me was that after 20 years of a completely secular life in mainstream show business, she wanted somebody to talk to her about Jesus. She said to me in our first meeting, "Frankly, I'm just exhausted with unbelief. I just can't keep it up anymore."

The [September 11, 2001, terrorist attacks] certainly played a role in this woman's search for meaning, as it has for countless others particularly in the American entertainment industry. But beyond the simple urge to seek answers to the murderous hatred of Islamic terrorists half a world away, this woman was reflecting a positive sea-change that is sweeping through the American baby-boomer generation in general, and the Hollywood entertainment industry in particular.

After 40 years of being ravaged by the license of the Sexual Revolution, and just as many years rejecting any and all connection to any authority—whether it was the Church, state, or just the simple wisdom of the ages—there is a growing exodus in search of rest. They are exhausted with unbelief and its ideological stepchildren: hedonism, cynicism, alienation, isolation.

God in Movies and TV Shows

This exhaustion is being manifest on the sound stages and in the executive offices of Hollywood as a new openness to spiritual themes. A friend of mine is the creator of this season's biggest new television hit "Joan of Arcadia." When she pitched the idea to CBS, she said to the network executives with some trepidation, "Now, there is a lot of God in this show." The executives shocked her by replying with enthusiasm, "God is good. We like God." Believe me, even just four years ago, God was not "good" at CBS or any other major network offices.

All of the major prime-time dramas have been exploring more and more overt religious themes. Any prime-time special that features any kind of religious angle is certain to garner good to great ratings.

The cinema side has also been experiencing a spiritual awakening. "Bruce Almighty" was one of the top five movies of 2003. "A Walk to Remember," a positive portrayal of a Christian teen-ager, brought in a huge profit at the box-office. And of course, the box-office success of the "Lord of the Rings" trilogy and now "The Passion of the Christ" (which, in Hollywood, we all just call, "The Movie") are the stuff of industry legend. Other recent films while not being overtly religious, do demonstrate a profound rejection of the lies of postmodernism. Films like "In America," "Lost in Translation," "Changing Lanes," "In the Bedroom"—are just a few examples of this new exhaustion with the legacy of unbelief.

From a creative standpoint, this is a happy trend for filmmakers like us who unite our passion for cinema with a passion for God. Any producer can get a hearing from Hollywood right now if they say, "I have a movie for the audience who loved 'The Passion.'"

A Lack of Understanding

Of course, part of this is because nobody in Hollywood understands who the audience for The Movie is, and what it was about The Movie that they loved so much. One studio executive confessed his frustration about "The Passion" at a recent party I attended. He said, "I don't get it. Aren't Christians the people who hate violence in the movies? Well, this movie is a two-hour execution, and they like it?"

There is a warning for us religious filmmakers in this moment. While this new openness to spiritual truths is an exciting opportunity, it also carries a huge creative challenge.

The fact is, movies about transcendent realities, that are not really great works of art, tend to be really, really terrible. Movies about faith and spirituality that are not haunting and profound, tend to be insulting over-simplifications. Movies about the conflict between good and evil that are not intense and grueling, tend to be sickeningly sentimental and easy. Movies about the search for meaning that are not probing and insightful tend to be laughable and pretentious.

This kind of movie is best made by those who are mature as filmmakers and believers. One of the reasons "The Passion" is such an overwhelming film, is because it has both technical mastery and profound content. Despite Hollywood's eagerness to serve "the audience of 'The Passion,'" we aren't going to see another film like it until we see another filmmaker who, like Mel Gibson, actually believes this God stuff.

Rejection of the Material

Another reason for hope in Hollywood is related to the search for the spiritual, which comes down to a rejection of the idea of a completely material universe.

A hundred years ago, the greatest American poet, Emily Dickinson, made a journey through doubt and materialism to come to the conclusion, "This World Is Not Conclusion." She was talking about more than simply the notion of immortality. She meant that reality goes beyond the stuff we see, the material things that surround us. There is an artistic movement crowding in on Hollywood which is pushing this idea more and more. It is changing cinema, or in many ways, restoring cinema to its roots in the lyrical, poetic imagery of the Silent Screen.

I call this movement the "Don't Show How Things Look,

Tell Us What They Mean" Movement. It is being driven very much by a young crop of directors who made their way into the business through the music video world. Music video is all about what things mean, as opposed to how they look.

Affirming Religious Values

Conventional wisdom used to argue that controversy kills any movie with religious themes, thereby discouraging projects with powerful spiritual messages that inevitably will look controversial to someone. *The Passion of the Christ* teaches future filmmakers that they need not feel timid about affirming religious values out of fear of public conflict; in fact, they might even welcome such attacks as a means of winning attention.

Michael Medved, *USA Today*, March 14, 2004.

The best music video directors freely distort real colors, shapes, dimensions and points of view, in an effort to complement and interpret a song. Rejecting the gritty demand for realism of the baby-boomer filmmakers, these young filmmakers are pushing for a cinematic lyricism that could mirror and echo the emotional power of music. Films that reflect this movement include "Donnie Darko," "Levity" and TV shows like HBO's "Carnivale."

The films we are starting to see from this new generation tends to reject the suggestion that limitless sex leads to freedom or happiness. They tend to have a sadness about relationships that is appropriate considering what they have been through as the children of "sexually liberated" parents. My friend, screenwriter Craig Detweiler, calls these filmmakers "a generation in exile, singing sad songs of Jerusalem." Films that exemplify this movement are "Lost in Translation" and "Eternal Sunshine of the Spotless Mind."

This is a great opportunity for the Church. We are all about the sacramental sense in which everything we see points to a reality we can't see. Chesterton said that, "The secular writer is confined to what he sees. The Christian writer speaks about what is really there."

It is for us to respond to this new generation of filmmakers yearning for meaning. We need our theologians and then educators to translate the "theology of the body" for the creative community, so they can bring it to their art, and then expand our understanding, in the way that Pope John Paul II has called art "a source of theology."

Power of "The Passion"

Undeniably, the release and astounding global success of Mel Gibson's "The Passion of the Christ" has been the most significant event for the Church in Hollywood and in cinema probably ever. "The Movie" has everybody in the industry rethinking many long-standing assumptions about the global audience.

It has many people in the Church rethinking their long-held assumptions about screen violence and the potential power for good of cinema. It is outside my scope to spend too much time here on this, but I do want to run down some of the ways the movie is opening doors in Hollywood and in the Church that could be very positive in the long term.

Three days before "The Passion" opened in the States, the industry trade magazines predicted, "This movie might even make $30 million in its first week." Actually, the movie made $27 million on its first day. It went on to make $127 million in its first week.

The main impact of the film in the industry is that it has created an awareness that there are huge numbers of people out there who went to this movie, but who generally don't go to the theaters. How to get "the audience of 'The Passion'" back to the theaters is now an agenda item for all the studios. Of course, they don't know what we Christians want to see, but they will be open now to create product for our consumption. This is probably good.

I never thought I would live to see Jesus, beautifully and devoutly rendered, carrying his cross on network television. I was astounded every time I saw a commercial for The Movie run at any hour of the day. I was at a restaurant with some friends one night and they had a television over the bar. Suddenly, an ad for "The Passion" came on, and everyone in the bar fell silent in a weird kind of awe and respect. I started to cry.

Beyond the power of the film itself, "The Passion" brought God out of our churches and into the center of mainstream culture. He was front and center, in his most compelling posture as Lamb of God, and many millions of his sheep heard his voice—some for the first time.

Undeniably, this has been an opportunity for dialogue and evangelization that the Church has rarely experienced before. As the Pope has said, "The Church would be sadly remiss" if she were to ignore the potential of the cultural marketplace, and I would add especially after "The Passion" phenomenon. . . .

What's Needed from the Church

I was interviewed by the magazine of the Writers Guild of America. The reporter asked me, "What do Christians bring to the table in Hollywood, such that, we non-Christians would miss if you were gone?"

It is a great question that Christians in every discipline need to ask themselves. "What defines a Christian as a doctor? As a scientist? As a teacher?" If our faith is true, it has something to say about every aspect of human life.

I have noted above, that the Church can help the industry find real meaning for realities like human sexuality, violence, good and evil, the yearning for the transcendent, human personhood, the importance of the family, etc. I want to end with two specific things that the secular industry needs from the Church, that, to answer the question of the journalist last year, will be sadly missing from the world of entertainment if we do not bring them to the fore.

Spirituality for Artists

The first is a specific spirituality for artists. There are very specific spiritual challenges that creative people have to go through to bring, what the Pope calls, "new epiphanies of beauty" into the world. Their first cross is their craft which will demand many sacrifices of time, labor, study, isolation.

In order to bring beauty into the world, an artist will have to descend to the darkest, loneliest places in themselves. Their art will have more power insofar as it is, what writer Flannery O'Connor called, "A wrestling with their angels and demons, not certain if they will come out of the struggle at all."

Artists have to abide in the suffering of insufficiency, that the work of their hands is never as potent as was their original vision. Their lives will be characterized by instability, poverty and then possibly the burden of celebrity. In an average year, a professional actor, writer, singer or artist will face more rejection than most people do in their lifetime. It is a lonely and painful process especially because artists tend to be more sensitive souls as it is. Many of them find ways to cope in drugs, sex, alcohol, because they have no Jesus to whom they could bring their burden.

We need to help these artists carry the cross of the vocation to beauty. We need to give them spiritual strategies, a practical theology, ethical training and then, we have to be big enough to let them be who they are—a little crazy, a little needy sometimes, but also the bearers of many wonderful gifts to the whole world.

An Ethics of Art

Secondly, Hollywood needs help from us in crafting an ethics of art and entertainment. Without giving artists a list of "Thou Shalt Nots" that they will just ignore anyway, we can still have an impact by reminding them of the huge potential for good that is in their hands through the cinema.

The cinema can make people want to be heroes. It can connect us to each other through the pathos of drama and the joy of comedy. The cinema can draw us into solidarity with those who suffer and leads us to want to make a better world.

The ethical question to put to artists is, "If you have the power in your hands to do all these good things, isn't it an ethical problem if you choose not to do them? Isn't that the secular man's biggest complaint against God—that he doesn't use his power to circumvent evil?"

We need to help the industry move from the famous "right to privacy" towards a sense of sacredness for the human person that is both the object and then the receiver of cinema. The Church could posit a definition of healthy entertainment that would flow from the desire to promote authentic human freedom and development. What kind of cinema helps humans grow? What kind of cinema coarsens the human soul and retards our development?

The corporate machine that drives Hollywood will never stop to brood over these questions, but the artistic community which also has tremendous power is hungry for guidance, and has a passionate longing to make a positive impact on the world. There are many opportunities for the Church in this moment. The only question is, do we have the energy, hope and pastoral love to take them?

"Producers and networks are falling over themselves to prove their alliance with the homosexual activists."

Television Promotes Acceptance of Homosexuality

Albert Mohler

In the following viewpoint Albert Mohler argues that television networks and producers, at the insistence of gay activists, are promoting homosexuality as a normal lifestyle. Mohler argues that since it is unlikely that Hollywood will end its promotion of deviant lifestyles, Christians should turn their television sets off. Albert Mohler is president of the Southern Baptist Theological Seminary.

As you read, consider the following questions:

1. According to Mohler, why did gay activists Marshall Kirk and Hunter Madsen believe that the gay rights movement was in danger of failing?
2. How does GLAAD influence television programming, according to the author?
3. According to Mohler, what changes to American culture will result from TV's normalization of homosexuality?

Albert Mohler, "Television's Fall Schedule: The Homosexual Agenda Advances," www.crosswalk.com, September 25, 2003. Copyright © 2003 by Albert Mohler. Reproduced by permission.

B ack in 1989, a psychologist and an advertising executive set out to redefine the homosexual movement. Marshall Kirk and Hunter Madsen outlined their plan in *After the Ball: How America Will Conquer Its Fear and Hatred of Gays in the '90s*—one of the most controversial books ever to emerge from the homosexual community.

Kirk and Madsen were convinced that the gay rights movement was in danger of failure, largely because homosexual behavior was so different from the norm and repulsive to most Americans. As these authors saw the situation, the homosexual agenda was going nowhere so long as flamboyant drag queens and the North American Man-Boy Love Association [NAMBLA] dominated the headlines. Unless something changed, mainstream Americans would continue to be repulsed, offended, and hardened in their resistance to the gay rights movement.

With this in mind, Kirk and Madsen developed a six-point agenda to advance the homosexual cause. At the center of their approach was one inflexible point—make homosexuality and homosexuals look as normal as possible. Their first commandment, therefore, was to "talk about gays and gayness as loudly and as often as possible." Almost fifteen years after the book's publication, it is clear that the approach is working.

The Gay Agenda on Television

If the portrayal of homosexuality in the upcoming [Fall 2003] television season can be described in two words, "loud and often" would be the right words to choose. According to the Gay and Lesbian Alliance Against Defamation [GLAAD], the new television schedule is playing their tune, pushing the gay agenda through homosexual characters and story lines.

GLAAD just released its annual analysis of LGBT [lesbian, gay, bisexual, and transgender] characters on television and declared that "this season's line-up marks a critical step forward in representations of same-sex relationships and families." A closer look reveals that this "critical step forward" for the homosexual agenda is an understatement.

In reality, producers and networks are falling over themselves to prove their alliance with the homosexual activists.

Groups like GLAAD work full-time pushing television executives and writers to advance their cause. They review scripts and demand character and story lines that advance their cause by portraying gays and lesbians in the most favorable light. Kirk and Madsen's fourth commandment, "make gays look good," has become a virtual law in Hollywood and on the television screen. GLAAD's latest report offers undeniable proof.

The report points to new shows like ABC's *It's All Relative*, a show featuring a gay male couple with a college-age daughter. The Fox Channel's fall line-up will include another homosexual couple in *A Minute with Stan Hooper*. On this show, "Pete" and "Lou" are two men who "own and operate a local diner and consider themselves married."

GLAAD executive director Joan M. Garry claimed these two shows as a major advance for her cause. "For the first time on a broadcast network, the real-life experience of thousands of gay and lesbian families will be mirrored on television." She continued on a personal note: "My partner of 22 years and I can finally look at our three children and tell them there is a family on television that looks like us."

Beyond this, Garry pointed to NBC's *Coupling* and CBS's *Two and a Half Men* as proof of "a summer of unprecedented LGBT visibility following the U.S. Supreme Court's decision to overturn sodomy laws in *Lawrence v. Texas*." She had every reason to be pleased. From the summer's *Queer Eye for the Straight Guy* to *Boy Meets Boy*, television is now pushing the gay agenda into America's homes.

There are still areas for development, insists Garry, for there are no transgender characters and only one new lesbian character in the fall's broadcast schedule. Just give them time.

The Power of Television

Homosexual content is even more explicit and pervasive on cable schedules, where "multi-dimensional gay and lesbian relationships are a staple of cable network programming" and homosexual characters are portrayed "in complex romantic and sexual relationships." Complex? The complexity boggles the mind.

A full analysis of all homosexual characters is provided on GLAAD's Web site under the heading, "Where We Are On TV." The characters—old and new—are listed by show and identified by "orientation" and ethnicity. It's quite a list.

Asay. © 2003 by Creators Syndicate, Inc. Reproduced by permission.

Television is one of the most powerful influences in the culture. The television screen presents what Hollywood producers, executives, and writers think will attract viewers. But, as the GLAAD report makes clear, the screen also presents a vision of what the cultural elite wants us to see as normal, as well as attractive and acceptable. They are winning.

GLAAD describes its work as "promoting or ensuring fair, accurate and inclusive representations of people and events in the media as a means of eliminating homophobia and discrimination based on gender identity and sexual orientation." They work at this with a passionate devotion to their cause, and with eager partners in the entertainment industry. Hollywood is now the center of an entertainment system that reaches into every American home in one way or another. In most homes, that reach comes through many avenues simultaneously.

The Future Looks Bleak

The GLAAD report was written as an insider document for the homosexual community, but it also serves as a warning to the rest of us of what is to come. America's toxic entertainment culture is going to be even more poisonous to Christian morality in the next television season. The natural family is now just one option among others. Almost any combination of persons will now be recognized by Hollywood as a family. Homosexual characters and couples "in complex romantic and sexual relationships" will become regular fare.

There is little reason for hope that Hollywood will be reformed—at least anytime soon. The entertainment industry is an industry after all. Writers, actors and producers will press the envelope, but the fact remains that the advertising slots are selling and someone is watching. We are on the losing side in Hollywood.

Christians—especially parents—must ask themselves why we would allow this propaganda for immorality into our homes. The most important part on the television is now the "off" button.

"By condoning the ridicule and humiliation of homosexuals in the media, TV tacitly approves their mistreatment."

Television Encourages Viewers to Reject Homosexuals

Abigail Graber

In the following viewpoint Abigail Graber argues that television programs that perpetuate stereotypes of gay people are harmful to gays and lesbians. According to Graber, these harmful stereotypes limit employment options for gays by portraying gay men as only suited to work in the fashion and beauty industries. They can also incite antigay violence by encouraging Americans to ridicule and humiliate homosexuals. Abigail Graber was managing entertainment editor of *Silver Chips Online*.

As you read, consider the following questions:

1. According to Graber, what negative stereotypes of gay people does TV depict?
2. What TV shows does Graber describe that present positive portrayals of the gay community, according to the author?
3. According to Graber, what societal changes are necessary before TV shows such as *Queer Eye for the Straight Guy* are harmless?

Abigail Graber, "TV's Portrayal of Gays Goes Too Far," *Silver Chips Online*, February 20, 2004. Copyright © 2004 by Abigail Graber. Reproduced by permission.

They descend on poor slobs like feather-boa-clad vultures, waving maximum strength everything, from hair dryers to paint peeler, in an espresso-induced frenzy. They fret over each split end on one hopeless loser's head. The merest hint of clashing wallpaper or—God forbid—'70s décor is enough to send them flying from the room, wrists a'flopping, in a fit of comical disgust.

They are the "Fab Five" stars of Bravo's hit show *Queer Eye for the Straight Guy* and the latest in a fast-growing list of pop-culture gay icons. In *Queer Eye*, a world dominated by facial cream and designer jeans, no outfit is too loud, no makeover too extreme, no stunt too "gay." In short, everything is and has always been absolutely fabulous.

Perpetuating Stereotypes

But concealed behind the fluffy façade of shows like *Queer Eye* is a disturbing reality for the world's homosexual, bisexual and transgender population, a group whose lives on the fringe are a far cry from fabulous. Though both gays and straights credit TV with bridging the culture gap, popular, gay-themed shows, including *Queer Eye* and Bravo's dating show *Boy Meets Boy*, perpetuate deeply-engrained cultural stereotypes while mocking homosexuality, hampering the homosexual community in their efforts to attain first-class citizenship.

Though the antics of the Fab Five keep the ratings high, *Queer Eye*'s very premise makes the show offensive. The show overlooks a crucial reality: It is not the Fab Five's homosexuality that enables them to transform straight slobs into the flavor of the week. Rather, each is an expert in his specialty. Kyan Douglas, the "Grooming Guru," has a degree in cosmetology; despite his floppy wrists and squeaky voice, Carson Kressley, the famously flamboyant "Fashion Savant," holds degrees in finance and fine art. Instead of publicizing these credentials, *Queer Eye* insists that the fashion savvy of its stars is intrinsic to their "gayness," a wrongful stereotype that plagues gays in their search for equal employment.

Harmful to Gays' Career Opportunities

Because their employers and coworkers hold preconceived notions of abilities of gay employees, homosexuals are harrassed in the workplace. They are often denied promotions or equal pay; in one case, it was suggested to a gay journalist that he was more suited for a different job: hairdressing. Only 13 states and Washington, D.C., have passed legislation prohibiting sexual orientation–based discrimination, and no such law exists at the federal level. Until employers stop discriminating against gays and widespread legislation is passed freeing them from workplace harassment, for TV to propagate the image of gays as inherently suited for narrow occupations in the fashion industry is irresponsible and damaging.

Living Stereotypes

Are the guys on *Queer Eye* witty? Yes. Funny and sharp? You bet. But is the show a step forward for gays and lesbians? No way.

The producers selected five living stereotypes to stick in front of the cameras, replete with stylish clothes, good hair, money to burn, and plenty of catty wit and sexual innuendo. The show enforces the prevalent idea that all gay people are upper middle class white men with money to burn—despite the fact that most gays and lesbians are working class.

Nicole Colson, *Socialist Worker Online*, August 15, 2003.

While the lighthearted interactions between the Fab Five and their clientele at least provide a positive example of relationships between gay and straight men, there is nothing similarly redeeming about *Boy Meets Boy*, an exploitative show that goes beyond ignorant stereotyping to deriding the very state of homosexuality. On the show, James, a gay bachelor, selected a boyfriend from 15 contestants. In similar dating programs, the audience is meant to mock the leading man's shallowness—it's a voluntary choice for people to participate in these shows and expose themselves to national embarrassment. But in *Boy Meets Boy*, the joke centers around James' sexual orientation, an involuntary aspect of his character unrelated to his superficiality. Not all contestants were gay, so he might have selected a straight man and been rebuffed and degraded for his homosexuality in front of the merciless audience.

Ridicule Leads to Violence Against Gays

By condoning the ridicule and humiliation of homosexuals in the media, TV tacitly approves their mistreatment. There is a serious breach between gays and straights that often results in violence—in 2002, 1,464 hate crimes were motivated by sexual orientation, according to the FBI—and that breach is widened by defamatory programs. The U.S. is not accepting enough of homosexuality for shows as cruel as *Boy Meets Boy* to air. Instead of providing viewers with shows that dehumanize homosexuals and condone their emotional denigration, TV producers should seek to foster understanding between gays and straights.

For their part, instead of flocking to *Queer Eye* and the like, viewers should note gay-themed programs with depth and substance. HBO's *Angels in America* is a poignant, darkly funny look at the gay community, addressing AIDS and repression. And though Jack on NBC's *Will & Grace* seems to channel Kressley on 12 cappuccinos, his character is satirical and a foil to the multifaceted Will.

For years the gay community has settled for any exposure in the entertainment industry, good or bad, while struggling to eliminate the misconceptions and spite that cause marginalization. TV should reflect the complexity of the gay identity and issues in that community. When that level of positive visibility is reached, perhaps Americans will be able to watch shows like *Queer Eye for the Straight Guy* and happily dismiss the stereotypes instead of subscribing to them.

"Pornography is moving closer and closer to Hollywood's spotlight."

Popular Culture Promotes Acceptance of Pornography

Dave Berg

Dave Berg argues in the following viewpoint that the now frequent appearance of pornographic film performers in the mainstream media is dangerous to society. He claims that television's increasing focus on the pornography industry promotes acceptance of pornography and accelerates the decline of American culture. Dave Berg is a Hollywood television producer and a columnist.

As you read, consider the following questions:

1. According to Berg, what is the significance of pornographic actress Jenna Jameson's recent activities?
2. How has the Bill Clinton–Monica Lewinsky affair led to greater acceptance of pornography, according to the author?
3. In the author's opinion, what evidence indicates that pornography is becoming acceptable?

Dave Berg, "Porn Goes Mainstream," *Washington Times*, November 4, 2003. Copyright © 2003 by News World Communications, Inc. Reproduced by permission.

B urt Reynolds got an Oscar nomination in 1998 for playing an idealistic pornography producer in "Boogie Nights," which portrayed in a very unflattering way the so-called golden age of the San Fernando Valley–based porn industry in the 1970s.

Mr. Reynolds had researched the part by visiting the sets of some porno films, and he emphatically told me at the time that the porn actors all wanted to cross over into mainstream Hollywood but that there "wasn't a chance" it would happen. They had decided to take the low road and could never come back.

Into the Mainstream

Hard as it is for some to believe, Hollywood has always had its standards, but lately they've become more like guidelines. Pornography is moving closer and closer to Hollywood's spotlight.

The most hyped new show on television is "Skin," airing on Fox and starring Ron Silver as a porn mogul. Ironically, "Skin" doesn't show much skin, but it does push boundaries that network executives would not have even dreamed about pushing only a few years ago.

Nineteen-year-old Olivia Wilde plays Mr. Silver's daughter. She has a different impression of the adult entertainment industry than Mr. Reynolds did. She told *Variety*, "Porn is such a part of our culture that it's kind of ridiculous that it's still viewed as an underground cult . . . consider it like the modeling industry, only more amusing."

HBO is planning to run a six-part documentary on adult entertainment called "Pornucopia." Showtime's "Family Business" will follow the life of porn star Adam Glasser in early 2004. Twentieth Century Fox will be releasing "The Girl Next Door" in March [2004]. The film depicts a former porn star and the boy who falls for her.

"Inside Deep Throat," a documentary, will examine the cultural influences of the most successful porn film ever made. The hit Broadway musical, "Avenue Q," features a number about Internet porn.

Perhaps porn's biggest foray into the mainstream comes from porn queen Jenna Jameson, who was described by one

A Multi-Billion Dollar Industry

Sadly, pornography is a pervasive, multi-billion dollar business in our country alone, with revenues generated from movies, cable and dish network television, magazines, books and other materials. *U.S. News & World Report* claimed that the pornography industry grossed roughly $8 billion in 1997 and continues to escalate each year. Just one example of the extent of this industry is that in the year 2002, 630 million "adult" videos were rented in the United States.

William P. Saunders, *Catholic Herald*, February 12, 2004.

Internet porn addict as a "cultural icon." Her book, "How to Make Love Like a Porn Star," comes out in May [2004]. She recently appeared on the cover of *New York* magazine and was featured in an E! True Hollywood Story profile in August. Ms. Jameson is on the verge of breaking the Hollywood barrier that Mr. Reynolds said six years ago could never be done. But Burt's so retro.

Ms. Jameson has signed with the video games division of the Endeavor talent agency, which represents Ben Affleck, Adam Sandler and Jennifer Garner. Her picture currently graces a three-story-tall Times Square billboard. Abercrombie & Fitch, Pony and Jackson Guitars have used her in ad campaigns obviously aimed at a young demographic.

Network television offered her "Who Wants to Be a Porn Star," a knockoff of "American Idol," in which she would have played a Simon Cowell–like role. She turned down the gig, citing her concerns about influencing young girls. At least she has higher standards than the networks.

So, what's going on here? Why the new more tolerant attitude toward porn in Tinseltown? One explanation is money. Web site subscriptions and fees account for $8 million to $10 million. *Adult Video News*, a trade publication, reported more than $4 billion in film sales and rentals last year.

But "follow the money" doesn't explain it all. I think moral relativism has never been more, well, relative. I've witnessed an unbelievable coarsening of values in the media ever since Monica Lewinsky became a household name.[1]

---

1. During Bill Clinton's presidency, he was accused of engaging in oral sex with White House intern Monica Lewinsky.

The Post-Monica Era

In the common era we'll call Before Monica, there were no references to oral sex in prime time or even late-night television. But in the contemporary After Monica era, the floodgates have opened. I remember having a spirited discussion with a mainstream comedian who wanted to use the "bj" word on a late-night show. I suggested to him that the word was inappropriate on national television. He was incredulous, and sarcastically asked me if I had read the numerous newspaper articles about Monica.

Today, many high school students say that oral sex is not sex. They obviously don't remember ancient history during Before Monica. Perhaps the students were influenced by Bill Clinton or MTV, but they may have also watched programs on E! or VH1, which have featured porn stars on shows aimed at young people.

The new mainstream acceptance of porn is particularly dangerous because some of the most authoritative conservative voices, who would have spoken out, have been weakened for now: the pope and other Catholic leaders, Bill Bennett and Rush Limbaugh. As a result, there seems to be little awareness that a hideous trend is building up in Hollywood and mainstream media.

The thieves who have been stealing our children's innocence are no longer doing it in the shadows. They're now operating in broad daylight.

"Fox cancelled Skin *. . . for lack of interest."*

Acceptance of Pornography May Be Decreasing

Elizabeth Nickson

In the following viewpoint Elizabeth Nickson argues that some recent developments indicate that the pervasive presence of pornography in popular culture may be beginning to decline. She points out that a new TV program that glamorized a pornographer was cancelled due to lack of interest. In addition, Nickson claims that some liberal observers have criticized the impact of pornography on culture. Although pornography remains pervasive in popular culture, Nickson suggests that these developments are a sign of hope that acceptance of pornography may be decreasing. Elizabeth Nickson is a writer and columnist for the *National Post*.

As you read, consider the following questions:
1. According to Nickson, what is the significance of Martin Amis's comments criticizing pornography?
2. Why does writer Naomi Wolf believe pornography is so damaging, according to the author?
3. As cited by the author, how many pornographic movies are made each year?

Elizabeth Nickson, "Is Porn Beginning to Beat a Retreat?" *National Post*, November 14, 2003. Copyright © 2003 by National Post Company, a CanWest Partnership. Reproduced by permission.

Next Tuesday [November 18, 2003, the release date of the CD *In the Zone*] may mark a turning point in the pornification of everything. Will Britney Spears's core audience, eight-year-old girls, love their goddess in her current incarnation as writhing, sweaty, desperate porn queen or will they say, "euwgh"?

They just might. Fox cancelled *Skin* last week for lack of interest. The one hour drama, set in LA's porn industry was a Romeo and Juliet story of two families, one father a pornographer who lived in a 58,000 square foot house and the other an ambitious attorney general. Their kids had fallen in love with each other. Guess which was the good father, the really good citizen, giving $80-million to the hospital? If you answered porn king, you would be right. Who was the adulterous ambition head whose son hated him? The porn-crusading politician.

Changing Attitudes Toward Pornography

We will never know how this improbability would have played out, because no one watched it. In a further retrenchment the same week, Tina Brown, erstwhile editor of *Talk*, *Vanity Fair*, and *The New Yorker*, and the woman who single-handedly created celebrity journalism, had Martin Amis on her cable chat show called *Topic A*. She and Martin Amis both agreed that the pornification of everything, the pervasive presence of porn on the Net and in the culture was a bad thing, a very bad thing and that something must be done. And Martin Amis said, "Women don't like it because it devalues something they hold sacred, the act which creates life."

Whoa! Let's back this up a little. Martin Amis used the word sacred? Martin Amis is so revered by the cultural elite that once when I told one of my English agents I couldn't read him anymore because he was so dark and hopeless and scatological, she told me to never say that in public. The implication being that my career would be pitchfork done.

Recognizing Porn's Negative Impact on Youth

In the same week, the lovely pouting Naomi Wolf, author, famously, of the *Beauty Myth*, and recently *Promiscuities*, which told the story of how she and her friends had lots and lots and lots of sex when they were young, wrote a cover story for *New York Magazine*. Wolf speaks on the rubber chicken college circuit, and on it she has discovered that porn is ruining the sex lives of college kids. Which seems incredibly unfair to her (and to me). Porn, says Wolf, is teaching young men and women "what sex is, how it looks, what its etiquette and expectations are, by pornographic training—and this is having a huge effect on how they interact." Men are seeing fewer and fewer women as "porn-worthy." Women, "far from having to fend off porn-crazed young men, are worrying that as mere flesh and blood, they can scarcely get, let alone hold their attention." Real naked women, to these young men, are just bad porn. The rot reaches all the way to pre-teens. Porn, reports *The Times Education Supplement*, conditions the emotions of even nine- and ten-year-old boys on sexual desire and violence.

No Free Ride

If we give the pornographers a free ride on our youth today, what is going to happen to them tomorrow? As a father of five young children, I am very concerned as a parent. Eighty-two percent of Americans agree. In using their common sense, they strongly believe that we need to clamp down on this pornography trend. . . . Today, we are declaring a war on pornography, and fighting the real threat to our families. We're calling on that 82% of the population to join with us.

Scott Dow, War on Pornography press conference, July 5, 2004.

The male libido, holds Wolf, has been turned off the real thing. Furthermore, she observes that on these campuses, given the shadow play that sex has become, a very real, sharp loneliness defines the relationship between the sexes, that the prevailing presence of porn, with its brutal short satisfactions has eliminated the face-to-face eroticism of real relationships.

Social conservatives have, of course, been saying this for quite some time, but let's face it, until Martin Amis, Tina Brown and Naomi Wolf say precisely the same thing, nothing will happen. The unholy conjunction of porn, entertainment and money, is a juggernaut that no one can stand down without all of civil society finally saying hang on a minute.

Hollywood Hasn't Abandoned Porn Quite Yet

Despite the failure of *Skin*, Hollywood is ramping up the following: HBO's *Pornucopia: Going Down in the Valley*, Brian Grazer's *Inside Deep Throat*, Showtimes' *Family Business* (porn business), Regency's *The Girl Next Door* (porn star), a sex advice book from the Vivid Girls, and porn queen Jenna Jameson's *How to Make Love Like a Porn Star*, out in May [2004]. In January a reality/porn TV show called *Can You Be a Porn Star?* will be launched.

There are, today, 260 million pages of porn on the Internet, up from 14 million five years ago and they rack up a billion in sales. Four billion dollars a year is spent on video porn in the States, more than on football, baseball or basketball. People rent 700 million porn videos. Every year, 400 regular movies are made. The porn crowd makes 11,000.

The seemingly blameless Internet portal Yahoo has clubs devoted to father-daughter incest, complete with pictures. There is, as the American Family Association has reported, a Forced White Wife Club, which "has photos of a man forcing a handgun into the mouth of a woman he is violating." There is an Asphyxia and More Club, featuring "photos of naked women hung by the neck, and others strangled by men." There are Real Rape Fantasies clubs. There is Rob's Necrophilia Fantasy Club, boasting "autopsy photos of naked women and medical-school cadavers. There is also a photo of what appears to be an emaciated concentration-camp victim lying naked in a mass grave next to a deceased child. A sexually suggestive caption is provided."

The thing about sexual desire and porn seems to be that the transgressive nature of the visual stimulus has to ever-increase, to get the punter off. It is as lethal and destructive a drug as heroin.

Hope for Change

In Canada, a group of Christian men and women have been fighting for the right to seize child pornography; only the Toronto police force has responded. In the U.S., the new

Child Exploitation and Obscenity Section has a staff of 50, including many attorneys who use child protection laws to curb child pornography. On both sides of the border, activists complain about lack of public resolve. Yet, Naomi Wolf, Martin Amis and John Ashcroft a big tent social movement make. But my money's on Britney's little girls.

"*[*Playboy *magazine] made pornography respectable and it helped mainstream it.*'"

Playboy Magazine Legitimized Pornography

Sheila Gibbons

Regardless of how "classy" *Playboy* founder Hugh Hefner claims his magazine was intended to be, it has wound up being a vehicle for men to leer at naked women, argues Sheila Gibbons in the following viewpoint. The magazine has helped to spread pornography throughout the culture and has denigrated women. Sheila Gibbons is editor of *Media Report to Women*, a quarterly journal of news, research, and commentary about women and the media.

As you read, consider the following questions:
1. According to Gibbons, why is *Playboy* not the sophisticated magazine its founder describes?
2. How are women depicted in *Playboy*, according to the author?
3. In the author's opinion, why do men buy *Playboy?*

Sheila Gibbons, "*Playboy*'s Legacy Is Leering, Not Liberation," www.womensenews. org, December 17, 2003. Copyright © 2004 by Women's eNews, Inc. Reproduced by permission.

S ome folks are fit and fun at 50. Some haven't evolved with the times. The latter would describe *Playboy* magazine, now marking a half-century as some men's substitute for dating.

Playboy still ranks 19th in circulation among U.S. consumer magazines, although at 3.1 million, its subscriber base is less than half of its highs of the 1970s. To build readership, the magazine seems to be trying to appeal to more kinds of readers: chaps who like cigars and cognac, chaps who like tractor pulls and chaps who are into video gaming. A disparate group, but no worries, mate: They all like naked women, the core of the original *Playboy* formula, the unchanging bedrock of the franchise.

All About Leering at Women

Hugh Hefner says that he started *Playboy* for urbane, sophisticated men who enjoyed sex and liked to look at beautiful women. However classy the magazine claimed to be, it still was all about men leering at women's passive bodies.

And today's *Playboy* has a Hooters-like personality, with unpleasant "heh-heh-heh" snickering about women's bodies from readers who write in and staff members who reply. The cartoons are dated and juvenile. It's like expecting to meet James Bond and finding yourself introduced to Beavis and Butthead. No doubt pressured by edgier, more explicit competitors such as *Penthouse* and *Hustler* in the 1970s, and later, *Maxim* and *FHM*, plus the need to attract a younger demographic to satisfy advertiser demands, *Playboy* has been dumbed down—if you can imagine that.

Photo History of Hefner at Play

The January 2004 "Collector's Edition" anniversary issue is a celebration of Hefner, the founder of the magazine and Playboy Enterprises, Inc., a multi-media company now headed by Hefner's daughter Christie Hefner. By looking through the issue's annotated pictorial history, the photos of Hefner partying down through the ages, the articles (and yes, the ads), readers can track his evolution from sweater-wearing entrepreneur to bathrobe-wearing writer defending personal liberties to permanently pajamaed caricature of the

U.S. playboy reclining in his boudoir. In many shots, the aging Hefner is surrounded by fetching young women, including his current half-dozen underdressed girlfriends, all young enough to be his granddaughters.

Hefner launched the magazine on a shoestring at a time when sex was under wraps in the United States. In 1953, the magazine's debut year, movie couples slept in twin beds. You couldn't say the word "pregnant" on the air. Hefner thought he could draw a dotted line from World War II pinups to publishing and develop a consumer magazine for males that would challenge conservatism in society and in media. And he would take women's clothes off to do it while claiming to keep the "romance" in sexual frankness.

"What we created with Playmates was artistic," he wrote in *Fortune Small Business* (September 2003). "We put the girl into a natural setting and introduced the suggestion of a male presence in the picture . . . there would be a second glass, or a pipe, or a necktie. It was intentionally a situation that suggested the possibility of seduction. Although it was kind of at an unconscious level at that time, the message was that nice girls like sex, too."

Little Changed from First Issue

Playboy's nude models haven't varied much from the formula launched in the first issue, which featured a clothed Marilyn Monroe waving from the cover next to a cover line promising "for the first time in any magazine, in full color, the famous Marilyn Monroe nude." The Playmates look friendly. They don't simulate sexual acts. They usually are wearing an article of clothing (small and sheer) and stilettos. They smile and look inviting and ready. All are young and nearly all are white. In the anniversary issue you can see hundreds of them—each about the size of a postage stamp—who have appeared over 50 years.

Scattered among the peroxide, the silicone and the thigh-high stockings are lifestyle articles and celebrity interviews. Every woman has known a man who said, "I just buy *Playboy* for the interviews." Don't believe it. No guy spends $6.99 ($7.99 for the anniversary issue) to read interviews. They are paying that to look at features such as the Women of Enron, a pictorial of nude employees of that symbol of corporate malfeasance, and other similar offerings.

Bringing Porn into the Living Room

The photograph was invented in 1839, and the word 'pornographer' entered the dictionary a mere eleven years later. Over the next 114 years, pornography was still very far from the mainstream. . . . It was a vile business in an underground market. . . . What pornography needed to be profitable on a mass scale was to be removed from the sexual ghetto and brought into the living room. It needed someone to adopt it, domesticate it, and teach it manners. As a mythmaker on the scale of Walt Disney, [*Playboy* founder] Hugh Hefner did for porn what Henry Higgins did for Eliza Doolittle.

Read Mercer Schuchardt, *Christianity Today*, December 2003.

Journalists on Fox News Watch in December (as well as those in other forums) debated *Playboy*'s place in the culture. "A dirty magazine wrapped in the pseudo-respectability of a few articles," the columnist Cal Thomas said. "A great magazine," said Jim Pinkerton of *Newsday*. "A great magazine? I don't think so," said Jane Hall of American University. The most prescient comment came from a media critic, Neal Gabler: "It made pornography respectable and it helped mainstream it. And now we see the effects of that everywhere." There's the rub: In the name of romance, Hefner destroyed it. He helped to take sex in media from extreme reticence to sleazy prurience.

Rejected by Feminism

Hefner expresses a mixture of bewilderment and bitterness about feminists' longtime criticism of his magazine, adult-only networks, Web entertainment, videos and Playboy Clubs staffed by women in revealing costumes. (Gloria Steinem's turn as a bunny in the New York Playboy Club and her famous article about the experience documented yet another way in which the Hefner empire exploited women.)

At the same time that the company is adding harder-core material to its TV networks and Web sites, the anniversary issue trumpets the Playboy Foundation's history of legal battles in support of birth control, sex education, reproductive choice and equal rights for women, which for Playboy Enterprises, Inc. seems to be as much cause-related marketing as social altruism. (It should be acknowledged that Playboy is not an uncharitable organization; its foundation has provided support over the years to defenders of free speech (the American Civil Liberties Union and the National Coalition Against Censorship), family planning (Planned Parenthood Federation of America), breast cancer awareness (Bosom Buddies, Inc. and Associates for Breast and Prostate Cancer Studies) and filmmakers, including producers of women-themed documentaries.)

Hef seems steamed about women's ingratitude about it all, saying in Fortune Small Business that by the early 1980s "the feminist movement had embraced a kind of anti-sexual, anti-*Playboy* attitude. It was the beginning of political correctness."

The Playboy Forum in the anniversary issue comments that "Sadly, the feminist movement was hijacked during the 1980s by a fringe element that felt that pornography [was the target], not the pious, subjugated women."

Religion certainly plays a role in subjugating women, and feminists continue to work on that aspect of personal freedom as well. But Hefner conveniently ignores the reality that the hard-core TV and Web offerings of Playboy Enterprises work against women at the same time the Playboy Foundation contends it is working for them, and his hubris doesn't allow him to see what role he played in the current pornography boom and its consequences.

Liberated women may indeed enjoy sex, but few enjoy stripping down for all to ogle.

> "Playboy *really does have something to do with freedom, and these days maybe that's worth remembering.*"

Playboy Magazine Is Harmless

Catherine Seipp

In the following viewpoint Catherine Seipp argues that from its inception, *Playboy* was harmless cheesecake rather than pornography. She notes that founder Hugh Hefner did not intend to create a pornographic magazine. Although she acknowledges that the magazine presents a distorted view of women's bodies, she argues that *Playboy* represents freedom for women rather than oppression. Catherine Seipp is a California-based writer who also publishes the Web log "Cathy's World."

As you read, consider the following questions:

1. According to the author, how does *Playboy* represent freedom?
2. What complaints does the author have about women's magazines?
3. According to the author, how is *Playboy* different from other men's magazines?

Catherine Seipp, "Living with *Playboy*," www.nationalreview.com, January 13, 2004. Copyright © 2004 by National Review, Inc. Reproduced by permission of United Media Enterprises.

I grew up with seeing *Playboy* around the house, although as small children my sister and I were ambivalent about it. The other day I was cleaning out the garage and saw some of these mid-'60s *Playboys* we'd decorated with our mixed feelings. We drew bull's-eye targets on the Playmates' butts to make them look ridiculous, and then added cat's ears on their heads to make them look even more beautiful.

When a friend lost his job recently, I gave him one of these old copies of *Playboy* as a present. I felt a nostalgic pull to do this because when I was a child, my mother was in the habit of buying *Playboy* for any man in her life who'd suffered a setback: My father's grandmother had died, an apartment manager was in the hospital, the handyman had fallen off the roof.

"It's just cheesecake!" she'd say cheerfully. And really, at the time this was true.

Then one day, she bought a copy and was appalled. I think the ailing apartment manager got a bottle of Scotch that year instead. But the *Playboy* I gave my friend was an old 1970 issue I'd found in the garage. The girls in their unsiliconed breasts—some of which are even covered by bikinis—now looked antiquely demure.

Pretty Mild Cheesecake

Playboy celebrates its 50th anniversary with the January [2004] collector's edition, and once again the pictures seem like pretty mild cheesecake. Yes, there's plenty of (rigorously styled) hair down there—and I kind of wish filmmaker Kevin Smith's wife had refrained from revealing her own little trimmed and shaved Hitler's moustache—but I think the pendulum has begun to swing back in that department.

LeRoy Neiman's famous Femlin, the little drawing that illustrates the Party Jokes, is once again pre-pubescent down below. And if that old "I read it for the articles" line is rather less convincing than before—I'd say Norman Mailer and Hunter S. Thompson have passed their sell-by dates—there's really nothing in *Playboy* now that needs to be hidden in a plain brown wrapper.

But then I know what else is out there. *Hustler* is disgusting. The financially ailing *Penthouse* is back on the stands with the current holiday issue, I'm happy to say (because I write for them, and they pay well), but I'd really rather not see photos of some guy's precious bodily fluids that have exited their source.

By the way, to proper feminists who ask how I can work for a magazine that exploits women, my answer is always, go write for a women's magazine before you talk to me about exploited women.

Boredom with the Macho World

What made *Playboy* stand out . . . wasn't its monthly parade of newly minted beauties, as smoothly buffed and well-upholstered as a 1955 Buick Century. It was its unconcealed disdain for the *Field & Stream* lifestyle, its utter boredom with the macho world of fishing lures, two-man pup tents and Hemingway-style rugged outdoorsmanship.

Reed Johnson, *Los Angeles Times*, December 3, 2003.

Lured by the prospect of what, ludicrously, always seems like easy money, I have occasionally over the years done just that. But after endless, snippy, sorority slambook-style negotiations—"And FYI, the editor said, why does *she* think she should get that much?"—and torturous rewriting until the correct women's mag tone (perky, smarmy, know-it-all, generic) is achieved, that fatally tempting $2 a word shrinks to something like $2 an hour.

At *Penthouse*, on the other hand, the drill always went like this: Accept advance, turn in article, hear back from editor within hours about how much he liked it, collect $6,000.

So, you know, I can live with my prose being surrounded by close-ups of some girl's rectum. But that's *Penthouse*. Anyone who calls *Playboy* pornography at this point is being willfully naïve.

Hefner's Popularity

The 77-year-old Hugh Hefner has a well-deserved reputation now as a dirty old man, which gets him much contemptuous ribbing from the media, and that's fair enough. But for the record, the hoi polloi think he's just great.

I witnessed this a few years ago at a Warner Brothers

Records party for Madonna at some grittily located dance club, and no celebrity got nearly as big a roar of approval from fans in the bleachers as Hef did when he showed up with his gaggle of blonde girlfriends. (I think he was with Brande and the twins Sandy and Mandy at the time, but he's since made his way through a bunch more: Handy, Dandee, Randi, Glandee and Post-Priandee . . . although I may not have their names exactly right.)

"Frisky, Playful and Fun"

When he was starting *Playboy*, Hef imagined a brand that was "frisky, playful and fun," as he put it, rather than dirty.

Hefner had originally thought of calling his new magazine *Stag Party*, but got a cease-and-desist letter from another magazine then in existence called *Stag*. "I was starting to have reservations about the name anyway," he said at a recent press conference. No wonder. *Stag Party* conjures up the sort of kinky '50s men's magazines featured in the new Feral House book *It's a Man's World*.

"*Swank* published new stories by William Saroyan and Graham Greene, and God alone knows who read them," Bruce Jay Friedman recalls in the book's preface. "I assigned the late A.C. Spectorsky to do an article on girl pinching. He did one on girl bumping which I rejected. He did a second version on girl shoving; I sent it back. He countered with a third, on girl tickling. I returned it and paid him half his fee. Years later, he asked me to join him at *Playboy*.

"'I am making this offer,' he said, 'because of your quite proper refusal to accept anything but girl pinching.'"

But what about the distorted image *Playboy* gives young women about their bodies? I know from experience this can happen. When I was about 12, I asked my mother when my breasts were going to get spherically round on top, like balloons, instead of just round on the bottom. "When you get a push-up bra," she said.

"But Little Annie Fanny doesn't wear any bra at all and hers are shaped *exactly* like balloons!"

"Because she's a cartoon." Oh. Well, that was a disappointment, but I got over it.

It's easy to make fun of *Playboy*. And indeed there's something faintly ridiculous about seeing Drew Carey rattle on about freedom and women's empowerment, as he did at the anniversary party, while Hef strained to hear and his Playmate companions nodded sagely.

Except *Playboy* really does have something to do with freedom, and these days maybe that's worth remembering. A society that allows *Playboy* is not a society that allows women to be stoned to death for adultery. Human nature being what it is, we're probably stuck with either burkas or naked balloon breasts forever. I know which I prefer.

Periodical Bibliography

The following articles have been selected to supplement the diverse views presented in this chapter.

L. Brent Bozell III | "Mainstream Media Doing Its Best to Legitimize Citizens of Pornville," *Insight on the News*, June 25, 2001.

Patrick J. Buchanan | "Mel Gibson's Triumph," March 3, 2004. www.worldnetdaily.com.

William F. Buckley | "Porn, Pervasive Presence: The Creepy Wallpaper of Our Daily Lives," *National Review*, November 19, 2001.

Jerry Falwell | "Hollywood Still Maligning Christians," May 14, 2004. www.bpnews.net.

Paula Fredriksen | "The Gospel According to Gibson—Mad Mel," *New Republic*, July 28, 2003.

Gromer Jeffers Jr. | "Gay Republicans to Fight the Religious Right on TV," *Dallas Morning News*, June 3, 2004.

Michael Medved | "The Passion and the Prejudice," *Christianity Today*, March 2004.

James Poniewozik | "TV's Coming-Out Party: Gay Characters Have Quietly Become Hot. Can Their Love Lives?" *Time*, October 25, 1999.

Read Mercer Schuchardt | "Hugh Hefner's Hollow Victory: How the Playboy Magnate Won the Culture War, Lost His Soul, and Left Us with a Mess to Clean Up," *Christianity Today*, December 2003.

Bruce Walker | "A Tale of Two Hollywoods," October 14, 2003. www.americandaily.com.

Kyle Williams | "It's Open Season on Christianity," February 28, 2004. www.worldnetdaily.com.

Kenneth L. Woodward | "*The Passion*'s Passionate Despisers," *First Things*, June/July 2004.

For Further Discussion

Chapter 1

1. Heather Havrilesky argues that reality TV programs often have more interesting characters than do conventional dramas or comedies. Do you agree? If not, why? If so, is this the result of the superiority of the reality TV genre or a temporary shortage of well-written fictional TV characters? Does the fact that Heather Havrilesky is a TV critic lend more weight to her opinion?

2. Jack Thompson argues that violent video games, which he claims are being sold to children, are dangerous because they can inspire violent behavior. Why does he believe these games are more influential than depictions of violence in other entertainment media? Do you agree or disagree? As you formulate your answer, consider Thom Gillespie's belief that violent video games have redeeming social value.

3. Carl S. Taylor and Virgil Taylor argue that rap music is a more honest depiction of reality than other musical genres. Can this claim be reconciled with John McWhorter's assertion that rap harms African Americans? Explain.

Chapter 2

1. Jonathan S. Adelstein argues that there is too much vulgar content on television. What does he believe the role of local broadcasters should be in maintaining decency standards? Do you believe increased restrictions on television content is consistent with the rights guaranteed by the First Amendment to the Constitution? Defend your answer.

2. Carl F. Horowitz claims that when cultural conservatives complain about television content, they are attempting to impose their religious beliefs on the entire country. Do you agree that advocates of greater enforcement of broadcast decency standards want to impose their religious values on everyone else? Explain.

3. Jared Jackson argues that popular culture encourages young people to wear increasingly revealing clothing, and that this will result in the sexualization of children and increases in unwanted pregnancies and the transmission of sexually transmitted diseases. Do you think this is reasonable argument or an overreaction? Why?

Chapter 3

1. Ed Donnerstein argues that media violence sends the message that violence is an acceptable way to solve problems. Do you

agree? Why or why not? Gerard Jones, in contrast, takes the controversial position that media violence is healthy for children. After analyzing the evidence he presents, do you think his argument is persuasive? Does the fact that he is a comic book author have any bearing on your opinion?

2. Ray Deonandan argues that at its best, professional wrestling can be viewed as excellent drama. In contrast, Jackson Katz and Sut Jhally claim that it promotes violent behavior in men and degrades women. Which viewpoint is more convincing? Why? How is professional wrestling different from other forms of sports entertainment? Is its impact on society different from, for example, professional football? Explain.

3. Brent Morrison contends that the violent lyrics in many rap songs inspire some of its listeners to commit real acts of violence. In contrast, Pat Stack argues that rap music is used as a scapegoat; unaddressed social problems lead to violence, he contends. What elements of each argument do you believe or reject?

Chapter 4

1. Don Feder argues that Hollywood is hostile toward religion in general and Christianity in particular. Barbara Nicolosi, in contrast, contends that there is a new openness to religion in the media. Which author do you find more convincing and why?

2. Albert Mohler suggests that the media is promoting a "gay agenda." Do you believe, as Mohler does, that the increasing acceptance of homosexuality is the result of positive presentations of gays in the media? Or do you think that increasing acceptance of homosexuality has led to more positive portrayals of gays and lesbians in the media?

3. Dave Berg claims that the mainstreaming of pornography is accelerating the decline of American popular culture. What evidence does he present to prove that pornography is part of mainstream popular culture? Elizabeth Nickson contends that the influence of pornography on the culture may be declining. What evidence does she use to back up her assertion? After considering trends that you observe in the media today and evaluating the authors' evidence, which argument do you find persuasive?

Organizations to Contact

The editors have compiled the following list of organizations concerned with the issues debated in this book. The descriptions are derived from materials provided by the organizations. All have publications or information available for interested readers. The list was compiled on the date of publication of the present volume; the information provided here may change. Be aware that many organizations take several weeks or longer to respond to inquiries, so allow as much time as possible.

Americana: The Institute for the Study of American Popular Culture
7095-1240 Hollywood Blvd., Hollywood, CA 90028-8903
Web site: www.americanpopularculture.com

This institute is dedicated to the art of semiotic analysis, or the analysis of the signs of popular culture. The institute publishes two periodicals. *Magazine Americana* features journalistic-style articles written for a mainstream audience by members of the institute's think tank and other select contributors. *Americana: The Journal of American Popular Culture (1900–Present)* features formal academic research papers targeted toward an academic audience.

American Decency Association
PO Box 202, Fremont, MI 49412
(231) 924-4050 • fax: (231) 924-1966
Web site: www.americandecency.org

The mission of the American Decency Association is to educate its members and the general public on matters of decency and to initiate, promote, encourage and coordinate activity designed to safeguard and advance public morality consistent with biblical Christianity. The association organizes boycott campaigns against indecency in the media. In addition to publishing articles about controversial content in the media, it maintains an archive of past issues of its monthly newsletter *Frontline*.

American Film Institute (AFI)
2021 N. Western Ave., Los Angeles, CA 90027-1657
(323) 856-7600 • fax: (323) 467-4578
Web site: www.afi.com

AFI is a national institute providing leadership in screen education and the recognition and celebration of excellence in the art of film, television, and digital media. As technology has advanced, AFI has expanded its purview to encompass all aspects of the moving image arts. A great deal of information about the film industry is available through its press releases and reports.

Electronic Frontier Foundation (EFF)
454 Shotwell St., San Francisco, CA 94110
(415) 436-9333 • fax: (415) 436-9993
Web site: www.eff.org

EFF is a donor-supported membership organization working to protect fundamental rights; to educate the press, policy makers and the general public about civil liberties issues related to technology; and to act as a defender of those liberties. Among its various activities, EFF opposes legislation it believes constitutes censorship, initiates and defends court cases preserving individuals' rights, launches global campaigns, introduces leading edge proposals and papers, hosts frequent educational events, engages the press regularly, and makes available on its Web site a comprehensive archive of digital civil liberties information.

Entertainment Software Rating Board (ESRB)
317 Madison Ave., 22nd Fl., New York, NY 10017
(212) 759-0700 • fax: (212) 759-2223
Web site: www.esrb.org

The Entertainment Software Rating Board is a self-regulatory body for the interactive entertainment software industry established in 1994 by the Entertainment Software Association, formerly the Interactive Digital Software Association. ESRB independently applies and enforces ratings, advertising guidelines, and online privacy principles adopted by the computer and video game industry. Information about the video game industry is available on its Web site.

Federal Communications Commission (FCC)
445 Twelfth St. SW, Washington, DC 20554
(888) 225-5322 • fax: (202) 418-0710
Web site: www.fcc.gov

The Federal Communications Commission is an independent U.S. government agency, directly responsible to Congress. The FCC was established by the Communications Act of 1934 and is charged with regulating interstate and international communications by radio, television, wire, satellite, and cable. The FCC's jurisdiction covers the fifty states, the District of Columbia, and U.S. territories. Its Web site includes archives of its annual report to Congress as well as the rules and regulations that apply to radio and television content.

Free Expression Policy Project (FEPP)

Brennan Center for Justice at New York University
School of Law Democracy Program
161 Avenue of the Americas, 12th Fl., New York, NY 10013
(212) 992-8847 • fax: (212) 995-4550
Web site: www.fepproject.org

The Free Expression Policy Project, founded in 2000, provides research and advocacy on free speech, copyright, and media democracy issues. FEPP's primary areas of inquiry are restrictions on publicly funded expression in libraries, museums, schools, universities, and arts and humanities agencies; Internet filters, rating systems, and other measures that restrict access to information and ideas; and censorship designed to shield adolescents and children from controversial art, information, and ideas. A variety of policy reports, white papers, and fact sheets are available on its Web site.

Gay & Lesbian Alliance Against Defamation (GLAAD)

5455 Wilshire Blvd. #1500, Los Angeles, CA 90036
(323) 933-2240 • fax: (323) 933-2241
Web site: www.glaad.org

The Gay & Lesbian Alliance Against Defamation is dedicated to promoting and ensuring fair, accurate, and inclusive representation of people and events in the media as a means of eliminating homophobia and discrimination based on gender identity and sexual orientation. Its Web site contains several downloadable research reports.

Morality in Media

475 Riverside Dr., Suite 239, New York, NY 10115
(212) 870-3222 • fax: (212) 870-2765
Web site: www.moralityinmedia.org

Morality in Media is a national, not-for-profit, interfaith organization established in 1962 to combat obscenity and uphold decency standards in the media. It maintains the National Obscenity Law Center, a clearinghouse of legal materials on obscenity law, and conducts public information programs to educate and involve concerned citizens.

Motion Picture Association of America (MPAA)

15503 Ventura Blvd., Encino, CA 91436
(818) 995-6600
Web site: www.mpaa.org

The Motion Picture Association of America and its international counterpart, the Motion Picture Association (MPA), serve as the voice and advocate of the American motion picture, home video, and television industries, domestically through the MPAA and internationally through the MPA. The MPAA developed and implements the content rating system in order to give parents guidance about the suitability of material in movies for children. The MPAA provides research reports about the movie industry.

National Association of Broadcasters
1771 N St. NW, Washington, DC 20036
(202) 429-5300 • fax: (202) 429-4199
Web site: www.nab.org

The National Association of Broadcasters is a full-service trade association that represents the interests of free, over-the-air radio and television broadcasters. Its Web site features a variety of data and documents related to the broadcast television and radio industries.

National Coalition Against Censorship
275 Seventh Ave., New York, NY 10001
(212) 807-6222 • fax: (212) 807-6245
Web site: www.ncac.org

The National Coalition Against Censorship, founded in 1974, is an alliance of fifty national nonprofit organizations, including literary, artistic, religious, educational, professional, labor, and civil liberties groups. United by a conviction that freedom of thought, inquiry, and expression must be defended, it works to educate its own members and the public at large about the dangers of censorship. Its newsletter *Censorship News* is published four times a year. A variety of briefing papers, press releases, and articles are available on its Web site.

National Institute on Media and the Family (NIMF)
606 Twenty-fourth Ave. South, Suite 606, Minneapolis, MN 55454
(612) 672-5437 • fax: (612) 672-4113
Web site: www.mediafamily.org

The National Institute on Media and the Family examines the impact of electronic media on families, and works to help parents and communities monitor what children watch. NIMF is an independent, nonpartisan, nonsectarian, nonprofit organization that provides reliable information so families can make prudent media choices. Its mission is to maximize the benefits and minimize the harm of media on children and families through research, education, and advocacy. Its vision is to build healthy families and communities through the wise use of media. *Links*, a newsletter, and a variety of research papers are available through its Web site.

Parents Television Council (PTC)
707 Wilshire Blvd. #2075, Los Angeles, CA 90017
(213) 629-9255
Web site: www.parentstv.org

The Parents Television Council was established in 1995 as a nonpartisan group, offering private sector solutions to restore television to its roots as an independent and socially responsible entertainment medium. The PTC agrees that parents have the greatest responsibility when it comes to monitoring the viewing habits of their children, but the PTC challenges actors, writers, producers, musicians, game makers, and advertisers to get serious about the vital role they play in shaping America's culture. Its Web site has a great deal of information about the content of television programs.

Recording Industry Association of America (RIAA)
1330 Connecticut Ave. NW, Washington, DC 20036-1725
(202) 775-0101
Web site: www.riaa.com

The Recording Industry Association of America is the trade group that represents the U.S. recording industry. Its mission is to foster a business and legal climate that supports and promotes its members' creative and financial vitality. RIAA members create, manufacture, and/or distribute approximately 90 percent of all legitimate sound recordings produced and sold in the United States. It provides a great deal of information about the industry through free reports available on its Web site.

Bibliography of Books

Joseph K. Adjaye and Adrianne R. Andrews — *Language, Rhythm, and Sound: Black Popular Cultures into the Twenty-first Century.* Pittsburgh: University of Pittsburgh Press, 1997.

Sandra L. Calvert, Amy B. Jordan, and Rodney R. Cocking, eds. — *Children in the Digital Age: Influences of Electronic Media on Development.* Westport, CT: Praeger, 2002.

Steven Capsuto — *Alternate Channels: The Uncensored Story of Gay and Lesbian Images on Radio and Television, 1930s to the Present.* New York: Ballantine Books, 2000.

Lewis H. Carlson and Kevin B. Vichcales, eds. — *American Popular Culture at Home and Abroad.* Kalamazoo: New Issues Press, Western Michigan University, 1996.

Leigh Clark — *Shock Radio.* New York: Forge, 1996.

Dave Grossman and Gloria DeGaetano — *Stop Teaching Our Kids to Kill: A Call to Action Against TV, Movie, and Video Game Violence.* New York: Crown, 1999.

DeVone Holt — *Hip-Hop Slop: The Impact of a Dysfunctional Culture.* Louisville, KY: Milton, 2003.

Stephen Hunter — *Violent Screen: A Critic's Thirteen Years on the Front Lines of Movie Mayhem.* Baltimore: Bancroft Press, 1995.

M. Thomas Inge and Dennis Hall, eds. — The *Greenwood Guide to American Popular Culture.* Westport, CT: Greenwood Press, 2002

Henry Jenkins, Tara McPherson, and Jane Shattuc, eds. — *Hop on Pop: The Politics and Pleasures of Popular Culture.* Durham, NC: Duke University Press, 2002.

Richard Kilborn — *Staging the Real: Factual TV Programming in the Age of Big Brother.* Manchester, UK: Manchester University Press, 2003.

Lucien King, ed. — *Game On: The History and Culture of Videogames.* New York: Universe, 2002.

Stephen Kline, Nick Dyer-Witheford, and Greig de Peuter — *Digital Play: The Interaction of Technology, Culture, and Marketing.* Montreal: McGill-Queen's University Press, 2003.

Kathryn Kolbert and Zak Mettger, eds. — *Censoring the Web.* New York: New Press, 2001.

Donald Lazere — *American Media and Mass Culture: Left Perspectives.* Berkeley: University of California Press, 1987.

Lisa A. Lewis   *The Adoring Audience: Fan Culture and Popular Media.* London: Routledge, 1992.

Eric Lichtenfeld   *Action Speaks Louder: Violence, Spectacle, and the American Action Movie.* Westport, CT: Praeger, 2004.

Jeffrey A. Margolis   *Violence in Sports: Victory at What Price?* Berkeley Heights, NJ: Enslow, 1999.

Eric Michael Mazur   *God in the Details: American Religion in Popular*
and Kate McCarthy   *Culture.* New York: Routledge, 2001.

Susan Murray and   *Reality TV: Remaking Television Culture.* New
Laurie Ouellette, eds. York: New York University Press, 2004.

Patrick Neate   *Where You're At: Notes from the Frontline of a Hip-Hop Planet.* New York: Riverhead Books, 2004.

Eithne Quinn   *Nuthin' but a "G" Thang: The Culture and Commerce of Gangsta Rap.* New York: Columbia University Press, 2005.

Nicholas Sammond,   *Steel Chair to the Head: The Pleasure and Pain of*
ed.   *Professional Wrestling.* Durham, NC: Duke University Press, 2005.

Joseph W. Slade   *Pornography in America: A Reference Handbook.* Santa Barbara, CA: ABC-CLIO, 2000.

Rodger Streitmatter   *Sex Sells! The Media's Journey from Repression to Obsession.* Boulder, CO: Westview Press, 2004.

Nadine Strossen   *Defending Pornography: Free Speech, Sex, and the Fight for Women's Rights.* New York: New York University Press, 2000.

David Volk   *The Tribe Has Spoken: Life Lessons from Reality TV.* Kansas City, MO: Andrews McMeel, 2004.

Mark Walker and   *Video Games: The Dominant Form of Electronic*
Michael Emberson   *Entertainment?* Norwalk, CT: Business Communications, 2001.

S. Craig Watkins   *Hip Hop Matters: Politics, Pop Culture, and the Struggle for the Soul of a Movement.* Boston: Beacon Press, 2005.

Arthur Frank   *American Popular Culture: A Historical Bibliogra-*
Wertheim, ed.   *phy.* Santa Barbara, CA: ABC-CLIO, 1984.

Jim Wilson and   *Choke Hold: Pro Wrestling's Real Mayhem Outside*
Weldon T. Johnson   *the Ring.* Philadelphia: Xlibris, 2003.

Frank York and   *Protecting Your Child in an X-Rated World.*
Jan LaRue   Wheaton, IL: Tyndale House, 2002.

Index